Making Sense of the Census: Observations of the 2001 Enumeration in Remote Aboriginal Australia

D.F. Martin, F. Morphy, W.G. Sanders and J. Taylor

ANU
THE AUSTRALIAN NATIONAL UNIVERSITY

E PRESS

Centre for Aboriginal Economic Policy Research
The Australian National University, Canberra

Research Monograph No. 22
2002

E PRESS

Published by ANU E Press
The Australian National University
Canberra ACT 0200, Australia
Email: anuepress@anu.edu.au
Web: http://epress.anu.edu.au

Previously published by the
Centre for Aboriginal Economic Policy Research,
The Australian National University

National Library of Australia
Cataloguing-in-publication entry.

Making Sense of the Census: Observations of the 2001
Enumeration in Remote Aboriginal Australia

ISBN 0 9751229 4 0
ISBN 1 9209420 2 5 (Online document)

1. Indigenous Enumeration Strategy. 2. Aboriginal Australians - Census. 3. Aboriginal
Australians - Population - Statistics. 4. Census - Methodology. 5. Australia - Census,
2001. I. Martin, D. F. (David F.).

304.60899915

The four forms in the Appendices are reproduced courtesy of the Australian Bureau of
Statistics.

Designed by Green Words & Images (GWi)
Cover design by Brendon McKinley

Foreword

This monograph had its genesis in discussions held over many years between CAEPR researchers and the ABS regarding the capacity of census data to adequately and accurately represent the distinctiveness of Indigenous social, cultural and economic life in its many varied forms. Initial discussions surrounded the correct interpretation of census characteristics in situations where these fail to capture the on-the-ground reality of Indigenous circumstances. Other discussions concerned the adequacy of census counts in remote areas following the publication of a CAEPR Discussion Paper by David Martin and John Taylor illustrating discrepancies in enumeration at Aurukun community on remote Cape York Peninsula. More recently, and following on from that paper, the idea of using CAEPR researchers (who were to be in the field at the time of the 2001 enumeration) as official observers of the census in select communities was raised with the ABS. As the case studies in this monograph testify, this plan was supported and subsequently brought to fruition.

This is not the first time that CAEPR and the ABS have collaborated to produce research of importance to national Indigenous policy development. In 1992, current CAEPR Associate and former CAEPR colleague, Anne Daly, was the recipient of an ABS fellowship which resulted in a landmark study of the labour market status of Indigenous people. In 1996, Boyd Hunter and John Taylor collaborated with the National Centre for Aboriginal and Torres Strait Islander Statistics to produce a joint ABS/CAEPR publication on employment outcomes for Indigenous people using data from the 1994 NATSIS. Boyd Hunter is also the recent recipient of an ABS fellowship under the Australian Census Analytic Program. In addition, several CAEPR staff assisted in the development of the NATSIS as members of Technical Reference Groups, and John Taylor is currently a member of the committee overseeing development of the Indigenous Social Survey. Over the years, ABS staff have participated in CAEPR workshops on employment equity, housing need, and the development (1992) and then analysis (1996) of NATSIS data.

In all of these activities, the ABS has displayed an interest in, and a commitment to, productive collaborations with CAEPR researchers. From CAEPR's perspective, the ABS provides statistical expertise, ready access to published and unpublished data, and, most importantly, insight into the methodological and bureaucratic processes that lead to official data collection. From the ABS perspective, CAEPR provides an interpretive and analytical capacity which is informed by ethnographic understanding, social sciences theory and methods, and familiarity with the social and economic realities of daily life in Indigenous communities. Together, these provide a powerful (and essential) means towards improving the quality of statistical information that is of fundamental importance to the development of effective and appropriate Indigenous social policy.

Professor Jon Altman
CAEPR
August 2002

Contents

List of figures and tables

Figures

Tables

Abbreviations and acronyms

ABS	Australian Bureau of Statistics
ANU	The Australian National University
ATSIC	Aboriginal and Torres Strait Islander Commission
CAEPR	Centre of Aboriginal Economic Policy Research
CC	Community Coordinator
CD	Collection District
CDEP	Community Development Employment Project
CFO	Census Field Officer
CGC	Commonwealth Grants Commission
CHINS	Community Housing and Infrastructure Needs Survey
CYPLUS	Cape York Peninsula Land Use Strategy
DAA	Department of Aboriginal Affairs
E	enumerator
HA	homelands association
IA	Indigenous Area
IES	Indigenous Enumeration Strategy
NACC	National Aboriginal Consultative Council
NARU	North Australia Research Unit
Q.	SIPF question
RNO	Census Record Number
s.	section
SIHF	Special Indigenous Household Form
SIPF	Special Indigenous Personal Form
SLA	Statistical Local Area

Abbreviations for kin terms (chapter 3)

B	brother
C	child
D	daughter
F	father
M	mother
Z	sister

Compound terms should be interpreted as follows: MB 'mother's brother', MMB 'mother's mother's brother', etc. When a compound term appears with one of its terms in brackets, this indicates that the compound term has different referents for different categories of people. For example (Z)C is the term used by a woman for her own and her sisters' children, and by a man for his sisters' children, while (B)C is the term used by a man for his own and his brothers' children and by a woman for her brothers' children. Anglo-Celtic terms appear in two forms: in italic (e.g. *sister*) or between quotation marks (e.g. 'sister'). The former are to be understood as terms in the Anglo-Celtic system, whereas the latter are approximate 'translations' of local Indigenous terms.

Acknowledgments

Paul Williams of the Australian Bureau of Statistics (ABS) has shown a continuing interest over many years in engaging researchers in open debate and in the exchange of ideas and information about the interpretation of Indigenous census data. It was he and John Struik, in his capacity as head of the Population Statistics Group of the ABS, who bravely entertained the notion of independent observation of the 2001 Census, and who made it possible. Logistically, numerous individuals also assisted in this process. Those deserving of special mention include Martin Brady of the ABS in Canberra, and Roger Jones of CAEPR who was invaluable as a constant source of ideas and critical comment.

David Martin wishes to acknowledge the invaluable assistance of Roylene Wolski, and the census collectors at Aurukun, particularly Albert Peinkinna. Frances Morphy would like to thank the enumerators, residents and visitors at community A, who accepted her presence as an observer with equanimity and good humour. She owes a special debt to the CFO, who spent more time than he could probably afford in providing information that could not have been easily obtained otherwise, particularly about the training procedures and the regional context of the enumeration. Lorraine Oakshotte and Sue Ward of the Darwin ABS Office also provided valuable assistance. Frances also thanks Roger Jones, David Martin, Will Sanders, Di Smith, and John Taylor, all of CAEPR, and Rosa Gibbs and Paul Williams of the ABS for their comments and feedback on various drafts of her chapter. Will Sanders would like to acknowledge the Tangentyere Council and Peter White, ABS Central Australian Census manager, for their assistance in carrying out his study.

Those who deserve special mention for their help with the production of the book include Paul Williams and Emma Perkins of the ABS for the speed and efficiency with which they provided the extra materials we asked for. Hilary Bek and Sally Ward of CAEPR are thanked for their copy-editing and proofreading.

1. The context for observation

John Taylor

This monograph explores some of the problems, successes and policy issues related to the application of the Indigenous Enumeration Strategy (IES) in the enumeration of Aboriginal people in remote parts of Australia. It is based on the evidence of direct observations made by three researchers from the Centre for Aboriginal Economic Policy Research (CAEPR) of the conduct of the 2001 Census enumeration in three separate localities. The localities— a major Aboriginal township, an outstation, and a series of urban town camps—were deliberately selected to be broadly representative of Indigenous settlement patterns across the remote north and centre. The aim was to sample a range of residential settings in the event that this variation had any bearing on the conduct and outcomes of the census. Access to the enumeration process was facilitated under the terms and conditions of confidentiality as specified by the *Census and Statistics Act 1905*. Each researcher was a signatory, thereby assuming official census 'observer' status.

Prior to the 1971 Census, relatively few resources were applied to the enumeration of Indigenous people resident in isolated localities, and the focus was very much on achieving a head count rather than a detailed profile of individual social and economic characteristics. Since that time, special census field procedures have been progressively devised, modified and extended by the Australian Bureau of Statistics (ABS) in an attempt to ensure as comprehensive coverage as possible of remote area populations, albeit within budgetary constraints. The direct cost of enumerating remote area Indigenous populations in 2001 was around $2 million (or $26 per head of population) compared with the direct cost of around $49 million (roughly $2.60 per head) for the total population. This cost excludes a number of associated costs such as form printing and transport, the processing of forms and the preparation of outputs (pers. comm. Paul Williams, ABS).

There are difficulties, however, in determining how effectively these monies are deployed in the pursuit of an optimal count and responses of good quality. The normal method of checking for accuracy in the count, using the post-enumeration survey, is not applied to the remote area Indigenous population. There is no standard test for the quality of the data on population characteristics, short of editing rules that might be applied at the data processing stage.

In remote Aboriginal communities, then, there is a need for close scrutiny of census procedures to assess whether existing methods produce optimal results, or whether alternative or refined methods are needed. These assessments, in turn, have resource implications of interest beyond the confines of ABS operational systems. For example, the Aboriginal and Torres Strait Islander Commission (ATSIC) considers that both planning and policy formulation begin with demographic facts. Indeed, the broad parameters of ATSIC's charter are determined by the size, growth, composition and changing location of the Indigenous population. These factors also provide the basis for assessing issues of social justice such as the recognition of need and the fair and equitable distribution of resources (Menham 1992: 37).

The ABS has claimed at times, on the basis of its own qualitative assessment, that the enumeration of remote area Indigenous populations may actually produce an overcount (ABS 1993: 6), yet analysts and other users of remote area census data have often asserted that the enumeration sometimes underestimates the numbers of Indigenous people. One particularly forceful claim, reported as part of a joint initiative of the Queensland and Commonwealth governments in the form of the Cape York Peninsula Land Use Strategy (CYPLUS), was that Indigenous people in Cape York Peninsula were substantially undercounted in 1991 (King 1994). However, this assertion was based on an invalid comparison between data from the 1991 ABS Census de facto counts of the Cape York population, and estimates of the 1994 place of usual residence (de jure) population derived from a variety of key informants in Cape York communities. To use the author's own assessment, it was constructed from deductive guesswork based on questionable assumptions (King 1994: 27–8). Such assertions of underenumeration provide no statistical basis for testing the proposition and serve only to obscure the likely underlying causes. Indeed, the validity of such contrary claims is difficult, if not impossible, to establish in the absence of demographic data that are directly comparable to those collected by the census.

It has also been claimed that the nature of census questions and the respondents' interpretations of them may misrepresent personal characteristics and patterns of social and economic organisation in remote Aboriginal communities (Ellanna et. al. 1988: 193–7; Commonwealth of Australia 1992; Jonas 1992; Martin & Taylor 1996; Smith 1992). Misrepresentation of social and economic characteristics can occur because the concepts underpinning the census questions lack cross-cultural fit. Data on income provide a good example. The census measure of income applied in remote Indigenous communities refers to a period of time—a typical fortnight—whereas the flow of income to individuals and households in remote Indigenous communities is often intermittent. It is difficult to determine what might constitute usual fortnightly income in many Aboriginal households. Intermittent employment and windfall gains from sources such as gambling, cash loans and royalty payments, combined with debits, for example due to loss of employment and cash transfers to others, create a highly complex picture even over a short space of time— one that census methods of data gathering are likely to misrepresent (Smith 1991).

Attempts to describe household composition provide another example. In census terms, a household is defined as a group of two or more persons, who usually reside in the same dwelling, who regard themselves as a household, and who make common provision for food or other essentials for living. Visitors to the household are not included. Ethnographic evidence suggests that these are highly problematic definitions when applied to Aboriginal households, particularly in remote areas.

While there is some utility in confining the notion of a household to residents of a physical dwelling or location, Aboriginal households are typically highly fluid in composition, often with a more or less stable core of residents and a variable periphery of transient residents drawn from the same community or regional population pool. In such circumstances, it is clear that co-residential groupings (even in the limited sense of who sleeps where), commensal units, family groupings, and domestic economic units are not necessarily coterminous; for example, people who live together may not eat together.

Commonly too, the basic economic and social units of Aboriginal societies comprise linked rather than single households (Altman 1987; Finlayson 1991; Henry & Daly 2001; Martin & Taylor 1996; Smith 1991, 1992), and what Aboriginal people themselves refer to as 'families' are typically dispersed across a number of households. It is such clusters of households, rather than individual households, which commonly form the basic units of sociality and consumption in remote Aboriginal communities.

The accuracy of census counts and of data on population characteristics, cannot adequately be established without reference to the particular circumstances of census-taking in remote Aboriginal communities. To date, a basic problem with the interpretation of census results has been the absence of well documented and fully nuanced accounts of this encounter between communities and officialdom.

There are some precedents for independent scrutiny of ABS field procedures. In 1981, two academics were invited to observe and report on preparations for the census count of remote Aboriginal communities in the Northern Territory (Loveday & Wade-Marshall 1985). This exercise focused on three aspects of these preparations: the organisation of field procedures and training of collectors, the pre-census publicity campaign, and issues likely to arise from the administration of census forms and questions. All information was gleaned from meetings convened by Census Field Officers (CFOs). The actual count was not observed.

While scrutiny of the preparations for the 2001 remote Indigenous census count also formed part of the present exercise, the intention was much more to focus on the conduct of the count at the community level, as well as on the process of house to house interviewing. The framework, then, is a critical assessment of the application of western census-taking methods in a cross-cultural context. Loveday and Wade-Marshall (1985: 249) found that preparations for the 1981 Census threw into sharp relief the difficulties encountered by the ABS in translating census questions into the context of Aboriginal society in various kinds of settlement and in remote outstation locations. For the 2001 Census, the ABS has acknowledged a need for feedback on census field operations, as well as a desire to be more informed about the social and cultural contexts in which their efforts are expended. This has been some time in coming, although as with all shifts in administrative process, it has an essential history.

Out of sight, out of mind: remote census counts before 1971

In many aspects of Indigenous Australian life prior to the 1970s, exclusion from mainstream institutions was the order of the day. In the case of the census, this was built on the 1901 Constitution, which at s. 127 stated that 'in reckoning the numbers of the people of the Commonwealth, or of a State or other part of the Commonwealth, Aboriginal natives shall not be counted'. Within this constitutional provision, Aboriginal people were counted, only to be then excluded from reckoning, although in the early years there was not even an attempt at full enumeration of Aboriginal people prior to their exclusion. The Statistician's report on the 1911 Census set the tone:

the full blooded Australian aboriginals…represent only those who were in the employ of whites at the date of the Census or were living in a civilised or semi-civilised condition in the vicinity of settlements of whites at that date. An enumeration of aboriginals living in a purely wild state was not undertaken (cited in Smith 1980: 30),

and

[f]rom time to time attempts have been made to ascertain the number of aboriginals in the various divisions of Australia, but the results have not been satisfactory, and the efforts in this direction of the Commonwealth Bureau of Census and Statistics at the taking of the Censuses in 1911 and again in 1921 proved disappointing (Commonwealth Bureau of Census and Statistics 1924: 951).

This comment on the 1921 Census is interesting: it was this census that saw the adoption of special methods designed to move towards more comprehensive and reliable population figures. This involved the cooperation of the Statisticians and Protectors of Aborigines in the States and the Northern Territory to arrive at an estimate of the total number of Aboriginal people, and their 'caste' and sex by administrative area (Smith 1980: 35). A system of annual Aboriginal censuses administered by welfare authorities was in place between 1921 and 1944, and it was claimed from 1933 onwards that coverage of the Indigenous population progressively improved with each succeeding census. In effect, though, for much of the twentieth century, the enumeration of remote Indigenous populations was more a case of mustering those administered by welfare authorities. As Smith (1980: 35) puts it, the 'practical difficulties' of enumeration were partly solved by the gradual movement of Aboriginal people into settlements—a process that was virtually complete by 1966 when the Bureau of Census and Statistics felt that, in conjunction with the Aboriginal welfare authorities, it had obtained for the first time a relatively complete enumeration of the Aboriginal population throughout Australia.

Thus, population counts essentially referred to individuals who were known to, and in regular contact with, welfare authorities. Numbers were presented by 'contact groups': those in contact with government settlements and depots, those in contact with missions, and those not in contact. This last group was classified as 'nomadic' and its numbers simply guesstimated. At the 1954 Census, for example, it was estimated that some 13,000 Aboriginal people were not contacted by census collectors (Commonwealth Bureau of Census and Statistics 1971: 7). By 1961, this figure was reduced to 4,000 and, as noted, the official view was that the 1966 Census was all-encompassing.

The referendum of 1967 and beyond

A census question relating to each person's 'origin' has been included in every Australian census since Federation, although the wording and format of this question have varied substantially since 1911 (Ross 1999). Before 1971, the origin question was structured in such a way as to ascertain each person's racial 'mix'. One reason for this was to exclude Aboriginal people (defined as those of greater than half Aboriginal descent) from the final count, as required by s. 127 of the Constitution.

The repeal of s. 127 of the Constitution following the referendum of 1967 was pivotal in the subsequent history of census taking. It was no longer necessary, for the constitutional purposes of reckoning the 'numbers of people of the Commonwealth', to identify and exclude Aborigines. However, as the 1967 referendum also had the effect of bestowing responsibility on the Commonwealth for (in Constitutional terminology) the 'good government' of Indigenous people nationally, it also provided a basis, or a demand, for the establishment of systems to gather statistics on the Indigenous population in an inclusive, comprehensive and consistent manner. Thus, the Commonwealth Statistician reported in 1973 that:

> For general interest, and in particular to meet the statistical requirements of Commonwealth and State authorities responsible for Aboriginal Affairs, it was decided that in the 1971 Census an attempt should be made to ascertain the race with which a person identifies himself (Commonwealth Bureau of Census and Statistics 1973: xiii).

The development of special enumeration procedures

In order to meet the new requirement for statistical data on Aboriginal Australians, the ABS introduced special arrangements for the 1971 Census in the Northern Territory and Western Australia. Over time, the system has been gradually modified and geographically extended and it now constitutes a multi-faceted Indigenous Enumeration Strategy (IES) that is an integral part of the general census operation. In urban areas, this strategy addresses issues arising from distrust of officials, population mobility and large households; in remote areas it is designed to take into account geographic isolation, high mobility, traditional culture, communication problems due to language, and unfamiliarity with form-filling. The focus of the present analysis is on the strategy as applied in remote areas.

Choi and Gray (1985) provide a history and evaluation of the initial steps taken by the ABS in its attempt to improve the enumeration of Indigenous people in remote areas at the 1971, 1976 and 1981 Censuses. Much of what they report is paraphrased here. They note that attempts to improve the coverage of Indigenous people in isolated situations (those 'out of contact') can be traced to the 1966 Census with the recruitment of Aboriginal welfare bodies, mission superintendents, station owners, patrol officers and police to assist in the count. However, they consider the outcome to have been less than satisfactory. Knowledge of the location of many Aboriginal people was lacking, too few people were allocated to undertake the count, and the personnel chosen were inappropriate because of general distrust of authority (Choi & Gray 1985: 5).

By 1971, the new requirement to provide comprehensive data on the Indigenous population led to the development of dedicated procedures for application in the Northern Territory and Western Australia. For example, collection districts (CDs) were created for the first time in remote areas to cover most missions and government settlements, as well as certain pastoral properties known to contain concentrations of Aboriginal people. In the latter case, letters were sent to station owners, through the offices of pastoralists' associations, informing the owners about the census and requesting cooperation. Where possible, collectors were recruited from station staff, while Northern Territory patrol officers and Western Australian Native Welfare officers were also enlisted (Choi & Gray 1985: 6). Some provision was also made for the first time to deal with enumeration problems among itinerant Indigenous populations in urban areas, although only in Darwin and Alice Springs. Logistical difficulties in conducting a simultaneous count over vast areas were addressed by commencing a population list one month prior to the census and adjusting for additions and departures at census date. Not surprisingly, this was found to be more effective in former mission and government settlements than in large reserves with indeterminate populations.

In the lead-up to the 1976 Census, the Department of Aboriginal Affairs (DAA) had been created, and responsibility for the census count of Indigenous people was centralised at the ABS in Canberra. As part of its expanding need for reliable population data, the DAA collaborated with the ABS in the design of special enumeration procedures for Indigenous people in town camps and remote communities, and input from the National Aboriginal Consultative Council (NACC) and other Aboriginal organisations was sought. Among the initiatives adopted were the use of Aboriginal census collectors in town camps, and the development of a special simplified questionnaire for communities where communication and literacy problems were identified. Flexibility in the timing of the count was also allowed in some Northern Territory communities in an attempt to accommodate significant movements of population.

Following a round of consultations with Aboriginal organisations and visits to major Aboriginal communities, the review of 1976 procedures recommended two significant changes for the 1981 enumeration that still resonate. The first involved the development of a special census schedule for use in interviewing individuals for whom English was a second or third language. The other was the devolving of central control of field procedures to the States and Territories, to take account of local conditions and to raise local awareness of the census. Over time this has led to some disparities in the implementation of the census methodology across jurisdictions, with the count being conducted sometimes on a place of enumeration (de facto) and sometimes on a place of usual residence (de jure) basis, and with individuals being recorded in a manner sometimes dictated more by expediency than by rigid adherence to the official methodology (Taylor 1993).

Enumeration by interview was pioneered in the Northern Territory at the 1976 Census and was extended to South Australia and Western Australia in 1981 (Queensland did not follow suit until 1991). In each of these jurisdictions, special CFOs were appointed to recruit and train collectors in Aboriginal communities, to promote pre-census publicity, and to physically locate communities (including outstations) to ensure their inclusion. In the Northern Territory the old system of relying heavily on police and other authorities for census collection was abandoned and a decision was made to recruit local Aboriginal people as interviewer-collectors in all discrete communities, with assistance in the major communities from adult educators (Loveday & Wade-Marshall 1985). A modification of the standard household census form was also introduced. It was broken down into separate components: a household form listing household members along with information pertaining to the household, and a personal form for recording the socioeconomic characteristics of each individual within the household. Information on these forms was acquired by interviewing a responsible adult member of each household. A Dwelling Check List form was also developed for use at the community level.

The benefit of devolving the jurisdiction of field operations is described by Loveday and Wade-Marshall (1985: 253) as enabling administrative flexibility resulting (in their estimation) in minimal underenumeration. Such flexibility included the production and distribution of customised pre-census publicity materials, the use of administrative records to fill information gaps, and return visits to communities where necessary.

Current practice

Subsequent development of the enumeration strategy in remote areas has essentially modified and extended the practices set in place in the Northern Territory, Western Australia and South Australia by 1981. Thus, the key operational features that set the remote area IES apart from the general census remain the use of interviewers and the administration of different forms with a modified format. While a systematic approach to interviewing and form-filling is outlined and encouraged in pre-census training, an ethos of local control and flexibility regarding just how the necessary information is to be acquired is also instilled. This can create additional idiosyncractic departures from general census practice.

The basic procedural structure of the IES is still as illustrated in Fig. 1.1, which shows the procedure for the 1991 Census. Using a Dwelling Check List (equivalent to the Community list in Fig. 1.1; see Appendix A for the 2001 Dwelling Check List), the first task of community coordinators (CCs) is to compile a comprehensive pre-enumeration listing of all dwellings in their community and to label each of these with a family name. Ideally, an estimate of the overall numbers of males and females assumed to be resident in each dwelling and available for interview should also be indicated. This process commences as soon as CFOs can organise and train an appropriate individual in each centre to do the job. Cross-checking of community lists with housing and other administrative lists is also encouraged. The method of compiling lists of dwellings and families may also vary according to who is involved, although this is generally done with assistance from council officials and other community record keepers.

Once constructed, the Dwelling Check Lists provide the basis for completing Special Indigenous Household Forms (SIHFs; see Appendix B for the 2001 SIHF), with one form for each household group (step 2; the SIHF corresponds to the Remote area household form of Fig. 1.1). In turn, Special Indigenous Personal Forms (SIPFs; see Appendix C for the 2001 SIPF) are completed (step 3; the SIPF corresponds to the Remote area personal form in Fig. 1.1) to record the personal details of each household member identified in step 2. The last two steps are, in theory at least, carried out by locally recruited interviewers in an interview with an identified household head—in effect an adult person with authority to provide information on behalf of all household members. In practice, the information may be supplemented from second-hand sources such as key informants and administrative records.

The process of administering each of these procedural steps inevitably involves a time lag with potential (and ultimately unknown) consequences for the accuracy of the count in terms of overlaps and omissions, especially in view of the high level of intra-regional population mobility in many areas. In recognition of this, fairly drastic measures are sometimes devised. In Yuendumu, for example, census day is brought forward by two weeks in those census years in which the real date coincides with the Yuendumu Sports Festival. This event draws large numbers of people into Yuendumu from all over central Australia (Young & Doohan 1989: 192–7).

Fig. 1.1   Procedural structure of the Indigenous Enumeration Strategy, 1991 Census

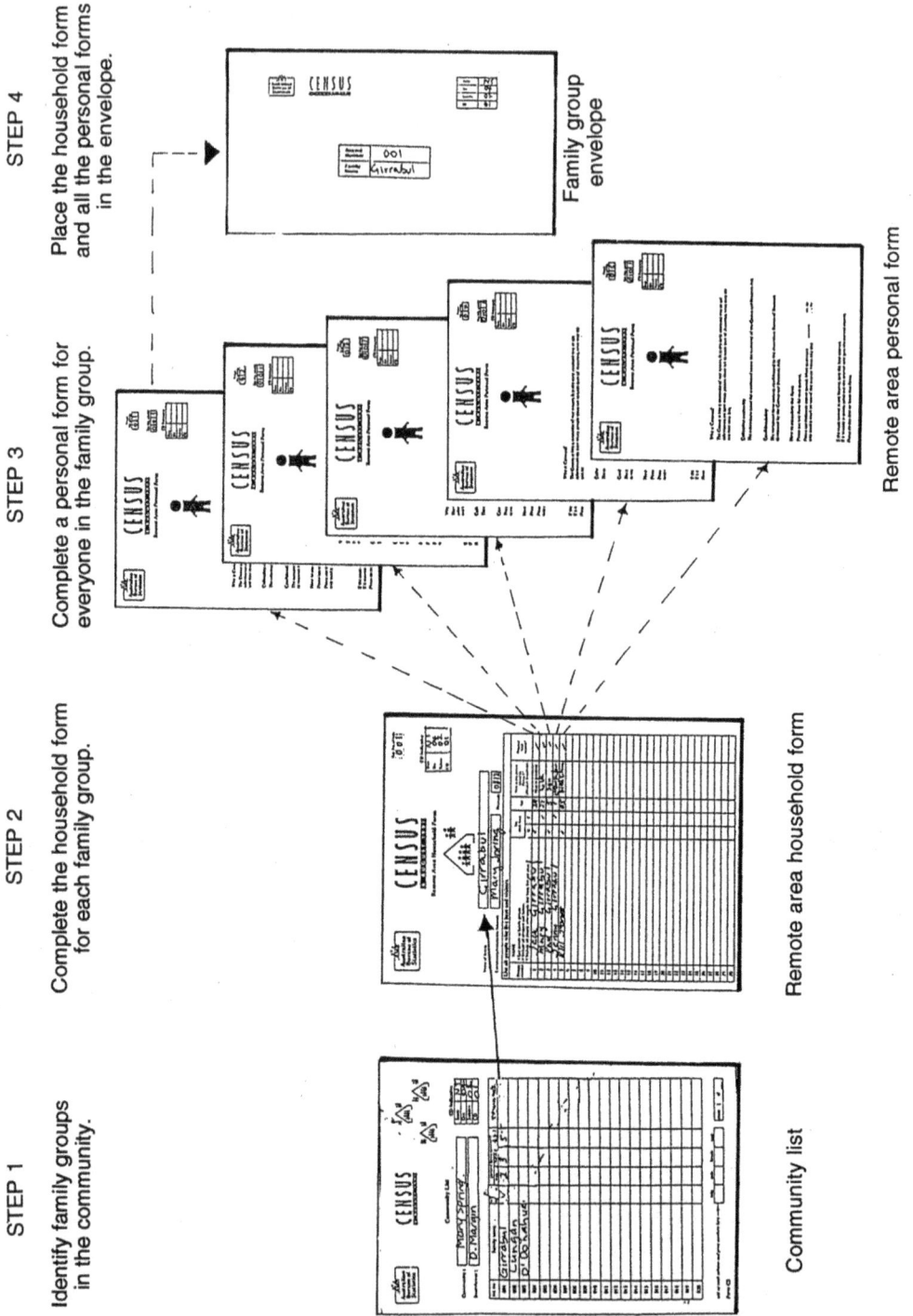

STEP 1
Identify family groups in the community.

Community list

STEP 2
Complete the household form for each family group.

Remote area household form

STEP 3
Complete a personal form for everyone in the family group.

Remote area personal form

STEP 4
Place the household form and all the personal forms in the envelope.

Family group envelope

Data quality

The accuracy and reliability of census data is dependent on success in these and other staged procedures—in the wording of census questions, in the design of census questionnaires, in field procedures for administering questionnaires, in the level of respondent acceptance of the census, in the nature of the responses to the questions, and in the efficacy of the processes for translating census information to appropriate and meaningful data categories. For each of these procedures, issues and nuances arise that may potentially compromise data content and quality in the final analysis. For a variety of social, cultural, economic, political, administrative, and geographic reasons, this potential is heightened in the enumeration of Indigenous Australians.

The criticism that official statistics inadequately represent Indigenous numbers usually makes reference to an undercount (Commonwealth of Australia 1992), but may also refer to an overcount, as in the case of Tasmania, for example (ATSIC Tasmania 2000: 3). Whatever claims are made about census coverage, there is no escaping the fact that the official ABS estimate of a 7 per cent Indigenous census undercount in 1996 was substantially higher than the figure of 1.5 per cent calculated for the rest of the population (ABS 1998: 28), and this was true again in 2001 (6.5% compared to 2.2%; ABS 2002: 4). While this undercount is compensated for in ABS Indigenous population estimates at the Statistical Local Area level, the ABS cannot make adjustments at the more local level of Indigenous Locations where data error is most starkly exposed. At the 2001 Census, a total of 62,884 Indigenous people, or 17.8 per cent of the total, were counted using the SIPF: the potential implications of any undercount (or overcount) that might arise from these special procedures are not insignificant.

There appears to be little doubt that difficulties in accurately enumerating some remote Aboriginal populations have persisted. The ABS acknowledges that enumeration procedures failed in particular localities in 1996, such as in the Anangu Pitjantjatjara Lands (Ross 1999: 62–4), and wider problems are suggested by often erratic community and regional trends in intercensal population change that may reflect census or respondent error from one enumeration to another (Taylor 1997). Specific insight into the possible nature of such errors is provided by a case-study example of the 1996 enumeration in Kakadu National Park (Taylor 1999). While it is true that variation in counts from one census to another may simply reflect the changing de facto population on census night, the Kakadu study found similar variation in place of usual residence (de jure) figures which one would expect to display greater stability over time.

Only one known study has approached a rigorous validation of remote Indigenous census counts (Martin & Taylor 1995, 1996). This concluded that there were systematic methodological flaws in the manner in which household membership was constructed using the Dwelling Check Lists and SIHFs. The result was an underenumeration, particularly of the young, the more mobile and the more socially marginal. Using ethnographic techniques to derive a separate and simultaneous count, this study estimated a census undercount of 17 per cent in the Cape York Peninsula community of Aurukun. While there is no basis for asserting that discrepancies of a similar magnitude exist elsewhere, the under-representation of such cohorts in official census counts is something that has long been noted by researchers (Gray & Tesfaghiorghis 1993: 84) and is routinely acknowledged by the ABS (ABS 1993: 16-17, 1998: 28; Benham & Howe 1994: 3), although no suggestions are put forward about why this might occur.

Departures from standard procedures

Clearly, enumeration of any kind in remote areas is a difficult task. Compounding the problems presented by dispersed settlement over large distances is the high mobility of the Aboriginal population in such areas. Furthermore, the geographical and social distribution of households and their individual members present definitional problems (Henry & Daly 2001; Smith 2000a). The obstacles presented to accurate enumeration by these and other factors help to explain the gap that is sometimes observed between official and unofficial population counts, and between the statistical construction of social forms and the reality on the ground. Such conundrums would be resolved to some extent if documentation were available detailing the method and practice of enumeration. At the very least, those using data would be more aware of how they were acquired, thereby allowing greater precision in their interpretation. There are several unique features of the remote IES that have potential bearing on the quality of census output and of which users need to be appraised. These provided a focus of attention for the field observations of CAEPR researchers.

For pragmatic reasons—the fact of high intra-regional and intra-community mobility—two of the most fundamental features of standard census procedure in Australia are effectively overridden by the remote area strategy. In the standard enumeration as applied to the general population, a self-administered count occurs on a single day—census day (7 August in 2001). In contrast, while referring to the same census day, the process of remote area counting can begin weeks before the day itself and continue for some time after.

The second departure from normal enumeration procedures concerns the nature of the count. The Australian census is, in the first instance, a place of enumeration, or de facto count. There is some indication, however, that the Northern Territory office of the ABS encourages a place of usual residence, or de jure count. At the same time it seems likely that a mix of de jure and de facto counting may occur in all jurisdictions since individuals are recorded in a manner often dictated by expediency. A complicating factor is the question of who constitutes a visitor to a household and whether CFOs and CCs make assessments on this matter in a sufficiently coordinated way.

Another departure from standard census practice is the use of interviewers and specially designed forms and questions. While it was not possible for each researcher to fully observe the training of census collectors, observation of their interactions with respondents revealed much about its effectiveness. Direct observation also provided insight into respondent attitudes to census-taking as well as a host of related issues. These include problems posed in acquiring the personal details of household members in often very public situations, misunderstandings about the nature and meaning of certain questions, the struggle to translate Aboriginal conceptions of the social and economic world into those demanded by the questionnaire, and interviewing difficulties presented by the ordering of some questions and the length of time taken to interview. In observing these difficulties, particular attention was paid to any trade-offs that might occur between an ability to achieve the fundamental purpose of the census, that of securing accurate basic demographic information, and the increasingly burdensome task of detailing social and economic characteristics.

The costs and benefits of devolving control of field procedures and decision-making to local units was also under scrutiny. Census-taking in remote communities presents a logistical task of considerable proportions, and very often this demands approaches that can best be described as innovative, or at least individualistic. In observing the playing out of these strategies, it was possible to assess the degree to which flexibility in an otherwise highly structured system either enables or enhances enumeration. Also highlighted are the sorts of obstacles that collectors face. One issue that these observations illuminate is whether consistency applies across the count, either as a de facto or as a de jure enumeration. The intent of the ABS, centrally, is that it should be the former.

The three independent case studies that follow collectively shed light on the issues outlined above. In each case, a common methodology was applied involving (where possible) observation of training sessions for ABS staff and interviewers, 'over the shoulder' observation of actual census interviews, structured interviews with CFOs, CCs, and census interviewers (and officials of community councils where appropriate), observation of interactions between interviewers, CFOs and CCs, and observation of the organisation and administration of census logistics. While styles of inquiry and reporting vary, reflecting different disciplinary backgrounds (Martin and Morphy in anthropology, and Sanders in political science), the studies complement one another to present a holistic picture. It is interesting to note that a high degree of similarity is observed across quite separate geographic settings both in the range of practical issues faced by census collectors in pursuing their task, and in the responses of Aboriginal people to the exercise. These common findings, together with local nuances, are summarised in a final chapter with a view to considering future options for improving the census in remote Indigenous communities.

2. Counting the Wik: the 2001 Census in Aurukun, western Cape York Peninsula

David Martin

Introduction

This chapter concerns the conduct of the 2001 census in Aurukun, a predominantly Aboriginal community of over 1,000 residents in western Cape York Peninsula. Almost all of the Aboriginal residents of the Statistical Local Area (SLA) are from groups whose traditional lands lie in and around the SLA, now collectively known as Wik people (Martin 1993). Fieldwork took place over a total of five days in Aurukun between the late afternoon of Sunday 5 August and midday on Friday 10 August. Roughly 50 per cent of the time was devoted to observing the conduct of the census itself. The balance was devoted to an unrelated project.

The region

The relevant SLA comprises the whole of the Aurukun Shire lease, an extensive area bounded on the west by the Gulf of Carpentaria, and lying between the Embley River north of Aurukun, and the South Kendall (Holroyd) River between Aurukun and Pormpuraaw. At various times when past censuses have been undertaken (e.g. 1986), significant numbers of Aboriginal people have been resident on outstations situated within the SLA. In August 2001 however, for a range of reasons including ceremonial restrictions on outstations and their access roads following deaths, none of the outstations were occupied. The conduct of the census therefore focused almost entirely on the township of Aurukun itself. However, a small number of people were resident in short term or semi-permanent dry season camps, most within a few kilometres of the township. Census collectors also made a special trip involving two days' driving to an Aboriginal-owned cattle station inland from Aurukun, on advice that several Aurukun people were resident there; in the event however, only two people were enumerated there. Quite a number of people had travelled overland to Pormpuraaw, a day's drive south of Aurukun, for a football carnival and had not returned to Aurukun as expected by the weekend before the census.

Demographic background to the census

A combination of reasons including the complex geography of this region, its monsoonal climate, poor regional transport links, and a range of historical and sociocultural factors, have resulted in there being a relatively low permanent Aboriginal population movement away from or into the area (Martin & Taylor 1996; Taylor 1995), although some Aurukun Wik people now live more or less permanently in centres such as Coen, Napranum and Pormpuraaw on the fringes of Wik country, and others live further afield in centres such as Kowanyama and Mornington Island.

There is, however, very high internal mobility. Ethnographic surveys conducted in February and June 1986, showed that some 35 per cent of the total Aurukun Aboriginal population had shifted their place of residence over the four-month period. Examination of household composition in these surveys demonstrated a frequent pattern whereby residential cores remained relatively constant, while more mobile groups (such as children and young men) moved between households (Martin 1993: 274; Martin & Taylor 1996), a phenomenon reported elsewhere in Aboriginal Australia (Finlayson 1991; Smith 1991). Who was considered a 'visitor', and who a 'usual resident', could be just as much a function of the social and kin distance between core household residents and the individual concerned, as of whether he or she was normally resident there. In such circumstances, it is clear that the census distinction between 'usual residents' and 'visitors' can be problematic.

Moreover, daily social life was characterised by high levels of movement, with most individuals spending much of the day either in their various work places or in more-or-less public spaces outside dwellings involved in socialising, playing cards and other such activities. It was often the case that residents were not in their homes well into the night, and that many dwellings would not necessarily have anyone present for most of the day.

Pre-census preparation

Preparation for the 2001 Census was complicated by the failure of the ABS to dispatch the relevant census forms to Aurukun. There was, furthermore, an Australia-wide shortage of the remote area forms, and so photocopied versions were prepared by ABS staff and air freighted to Cairns for onshipment by light aircraft to Aurukun. However, a series of unforseen logistical and other problems meant that the forms did not arrive in Aurukun until the day of the census itself, Tuesday 7 August. In the meantime, therefore, photocopies were made of the sample forms provided in the *Working for the Census* guide for interviewers, particularly the Dwelling Check List (see Appendix A) and the SIHF (see Appendix B), so that the necessary preparatory work could be undertaken. As it eventuated, because the photocopies were not colour coded as were the originals, considerable difficulties were occasioned for interviewer-collectors (henceforth interviewers) in the field since there was no simple visual clue as to which form was which, and in particular whether each SIHF had its associated SIPFs (see Appendix C) attached.

Steps had been taken to implement pre-census training. The CFO, who was based in Cairns, had conducted a training session in Aurukun, involving the CC and a number of the proposed interviewers. The CC was of the view that the training had gone well, although certain of the proposed interviewers had not attended. Although the video prepared by the ABS specifically to train interviewers in the remote area methodology was apparently not shown during training, this was probably of little consequence since the situation (including cultural 'styles') in the South Australian rural Aboriginal community depicted in the video and that in Aurukun were rather different. Of course, the difficulty for the ABS, and for those involved in census collections in remote Indigenous communities, is how to ensure appropriateness of materials and training across the range of communities and situations to be encountered, while maintaining consistency and commensurability in the data ultimately collected.

The CC had clearly put considerable effort into developing a methodology for census collection in the township at least, and (apart from the absence of forms) was well prepared. A number of potential issues had been identified prior to the census collection in meetings between the CC and the interviewers. These included the problem of how Q. 4 and Q. 5 on the SIPF treat kin relationships within households. In this regard, the advice from the CFO was that interviewers were to record relationships in the terms in which people themselves described them.

Problems arising from the 'married' terminology used in Q. 6 of the SIPF were seen as twofold. Firstly, the interviewers seemed prepared to accept that 'married' could encompass 'de facto', but were nonetheless concerned about the term's appropriateness; and secondly, it was felt that there could be people involved in long-term relationships but not cohabiting with their partner who might be concerned that describing themselves as 'married' could adversely impact on their welfare entitlements.

Doubts were raised about the wording of, and relationship between, the 'origin' and 'ancestry' questions (Q. 10 and Q. 13 on the SIPF). It was presumed that Q. 10 offered a 'no' option for those non-Indigenous people living in otherwise Indigenous households who preferred not to fill out a separate, standard, personal census form.

It was also felt that Q. 28, regarding the before-tax income of each individual, would pose difficulties for many people, since not only were people not necessarily aware of how much tax was deducted from their Community Development Employment Project (CDEP) and other pays, but also were not necessarily aware of the Local Government Services levy deducted by the Aurukun Shire Council.

It was felt that there would be problems in identifying precisely where people were living one year ago and at the time of the previous census, five years ago. The CC was proposing to use the Aurukun Council's lot numbering system within the township, but quite a few of the houses that had existed in 1996 had been demolished, and a significant number of new dwellings had been constructed in the intervening period, including over the previous 12 months. It was envisaged that during the actual census, the place(s) of residence one and five years ago might be recorded (for example) as 'Bill's place', and then a more consistent address system would be recorded on forms during the post-collection validation process. Additionally, neither the interviewers nor the CC were clear about whether the import of this question related to whether people had been living elsewhere than Aurukun five years ago, for example in other communities or on outstations, or whether it was aimed at establishing intra-community mobility.

More generally, the CC was of the view that there would be the need for several days to be devoted post-collection to the validation of information on the forms. It should be stated at this juncture that the issues identified by the CC and the interviewers all proved to be borne out in my observations of the actual census collection.

Despite efforts at information dissemination about the census, my own inquiries suggested that there did not seem to be much general awareness of it within the community. Prior to the actual census collection starting, only two of the dozen or so people around the township I spoke with knew about the forthcoming census, or even what a census was.

This is not however to be taken as a criticism of those involved in preparing for the census: rather, it reflects the quite different priorities and interests of Aboriginal residents of communities such as Aurukun, and a fair level of indifference to the administrative requirements and priorities of the state.

Proposed collection methodology

The proposed methodology involved dividing the township into some 11 sectors, marked on a map of the township provided by the Aurukun Shire Council. A total of 134 dwellings had been identified from the map for Indigenous residents. The map of the township was to be used to develop a preliminary Dwelling Check List for each sector. Those of non-Indigenous (primarily staff) residents, for which the standard census forms were used, were additional, and the CC undertook the responsibility of providing and collecting these standard census forms.

Responsibility for filling in and collecting the forms for the Indigenous households in each sector was to be assigned to one of five two-person teams of interviewers. The CC ensured that each team had at least one person who was fluent in or had a good working knowledge of Wik Mungkan, the *lingua franca* of the Aboriginal residents of the area, and at least one person who was competent to fill in the SIHFs and SIPFs accurately. In some instances, this meant that teams comprised a Wik and a non-Wik person, while in others one Wik person involved satisfied both criteria and was assisted by another Wik interviewer.

In assigning interviewers to teams, the CC tried to ensure that the capacity of each team to operate effectively was not compromised by personal incompatibilities between team members (such as those arising from kin-based restrictions for Wik interviewers), or by potential incompatibilities between interviewers and the residents of their assigned collection sectors. An important source of such potential problems was the high level of disputation within Aurukun, structured in terms of residence in the 'topside' (eastern) and 'bottomside' (western) areas of the township. As discussed elsewhere (Martin 1993), this basic division within the township reflects long-standing patterns of political and social relations between 'topside' or inland Wik groups and 'bottomside' or coastal ones.

The census collection revolved around three key individuals; the (non-Aboriginal) CC, whose main role centred on organising the logistics and ensuring the rigour of the collection, and two Wik individuals, one male and one female, who between them had an almost encyclopaedic knowledge of kin and family relationships and of household compositions across the township. Particularly in the case of the male Wik interviewer, the knowledge gained from being a member of the Wik community resident in Aurukun had been supplemented by his long-term role within the Shire Council administration. This meant that he had an unparalleled knowledge of the kinds of information which would normally be held in administrative data sets, such as household compositions, sources of income, income levels, information on employer details, and so forth.

The census collection operation was based in the large and secure air conditioned restaurant at the rear of the Council-run tavern. Tables had been set up around the room where paperwork for each sector was kept, including a copy of the relevant section of the township map and ultimately the collated SIHFs and SIPFs. In the hot and dusty conditions in Aurukun, having such a facility provided an invaluable aid in maintaining a systematic and ordered approach to the collection and its associated paperwork.

It was proposed that the names of those who were normally residents of Aurukun but were absent during the week of the census (e.g. at the Pormpuraaw football carnival) would be placed on the relevant SIHF. Largely blank SIPFs would also be created for them, and interviewers would attempt to get the relevant information over the two or so weeks that it was envisaged the census collection would take to complete. The strategy was clearly based on the assumption that absent usual residents would not be enumerated elsewhere, which at least in the case of those at Pormpuraaw was certainly justified. Visitors in Aurukun households were also to be enumerated.

It was also proposed that once all the SIHFs and SIPFs had been collected, an information validation process would be conducted, involving the CC and the principal Aboriginal interviewer. It was intended that this exercise would focus particularly on ensuring that children had been enumerated, working from the Aboriginal collectors' knowledge of who were care-givers and which children they looked after. Another proposed aspect of the validation process was ensuring that there had been no double-counting, for example for people who moved between two or more residences on a regular basis. The final stage was to involve 'spot checking', at places such as the community store, to estimate how thoroughly the census had been done.

Conduct of the census

The CC had planned for work on the collection itself to begin first thing on the Monday morning with the development of the Dwelling Check Lists. When no interviewers had arrived at the operations centre by mid-morning, the CC drove off to look for them. It turned out that the interviewer on whom so much depended, because of the unparalleled knowledge mentioned previously, was urgently required in the Post Office to sort the incoming mail (which included Centrelink cheques). The dearth of individuals with the necessary skills and education levels is a well-documented feature of remote Aboriginal communities such as Aurukun. One consequence is the high demands and stress placed on those relatively few Aboriginal people who do have the formal capacity (and the willingness) to undertake administrative tasks. While this individual was critical to the conduct of the census, he was also essential to a number of other concurrent and ongoing community administration processes. This was also true of a number of the other Aboriginal interviewers, for whom managing their work for the census also necessarily included taking account of competing demands on their time from other formal work commitments.

More broadly, the CC had to demonstrate considerable flexibility in managing the census collection process, including managing the work of the interviewers. Competing demands on the interviewers' time came not only from other work commitments, but also from within the Aboriginal domain, in terms of their involvement in the flux of everyday social and political process including commitments arising through formal and informal responsibilities to kin. Furthermore, the quite intensive and demanding nature of the actual census collection work was not necessarily in keeping with Wik attitudes and practices regarding 'work'. While obtaining an accurate census count and its ancillary information may objectively have been of importance, and this had been explained to the interviewers, it is typically the exigencies of mundane life which provide the imperatives for Wik people (Martin 1993). This of course was not just the case for the interviewers, but indeed for other Wik residents in terms of their participation in the census.

This inevitably meant that the only effective census methodology was to work within the parameters set by the ebb and flow of life within the township, and the CC was clearly very aware of this factor. One important consequence of this was that it would not have been possible to complete the census over the nominal census night of Tuesday 7 August, and like census collections in other remote Indigenous communities the collection necessarily had to be conducted over a more or less extended period. This of course has implications for the accuracy of the broader census—for example, given a highly mobile population in some regions, conducting the census over an extended period across a region may have the potential to lead to both double counting of some individuals and the missing of others.

However, it also has implications for the type of information collected directly by census interviewers in remote communities, since much (but not all) of the additional time required relates to the level of detail collected on each SIPF that is elicited from respondents, rather than (for example) from local administrative data sets. This in turn relates to what the central focus of the census should be for such remote populations; the basic demographic profile, or the wider questions covered in the personal forms. This issue is raised in the other case studies in this volume.

Effective and appropriate management of the overall census process in Aurukun therefore involved management of such factors as the periodic unavailability of interviewers, provision of proactive support and assistance to interviewers, and being able to direct the actual collections to take advantage of opportunistic lulls in the ebb and flow of community life and its priorities, for both interviewers and general residents. It therefore required a quite difficult balance between *flexibility* (in dealing with the high levels of mobility and the various exigencies arising during the collection process), and *systematicity* (in ensuring that the collection encompassed as far as possible all Aurukun residents, and that the accompanying paperwork, particularly the forms, was systematically processed and stored).

Compiling the Dwelling Check List

Eventually, by late morning on Monday 6 August, the main Aboriginal interviewer was able to leave his other work and come down to the census centre. Together with the CC, he worked systematically through the Shire Council map of the township, assigning family names to each of the dwellings in each sector for the purposes of developing a preliminary the Dwelling Check List. The 'family name' which he assigned was essentially that of the person whom he considered the most significant in the household, equivalent to 'person 1' of the SIHF.

However, in many cases a particular dwelling would be considered to be that of an individual who was actually living elsewhere in the township (and sometimes away from Aurukun altogether). Also, the 'family name' assigned to a particular household on the Dwelling Check List would often not be that of many or even most of the residents, who could for instance be in-laws, nephews, nieces, visitors, and so on.

A further difficulty was occasioned by the fact that the initial map provided by the Aurukun Shire Council was out of date. With the help of the principal Aboriginal interviewer, a quite significant number of vacant or unoccupied dwellings were identified and marked on the map. These ranged from derelict houses awaiting either refurbishment or demolition, to houses temporarily vacant under ritual restrictions following deaths. As well, houses constructed since the time that the map had been drawn up were marked and numbered. Even so, once interviewers started the actual work of filling in forms in each sector, a number of changes had to be made to the Dwelling Check List for certain sectors.

Filling in the Household and Personal Forms

Interviewer teams that I observed usually—but not always—started the gathering of information on the SIHF and SIPFs with statements about what the census broadly entailed, and of its significance in terms of getting an accurate count of the population so that Aurukun could receive the necessary levels of funding for housing and other infrastructure.

The teams had to be very flexible, and adapt their interviews to the flux of social life in the township. This meant working around the 'wages or welfare payments, alcohol consumption, conflict and dislocation' cycle to which Aurukun was subjected, like many other remote communities with liquor outlets. It also meant that if there was a group playing cards at a dwelling (a major social and economic activity within Aurukun), the interviewers would leave it till a later time, as it would have caused embarrassment and possibly hostility to interrupt the game.

The procedure usually started with the interviewer attempting to elicit the names and relevant details of residents for the SIHF, before then moving to the SIPFs. In some cases, the Aboriginal interviewer sat beside the respondent, filling in most of the information himself without directly questioning the respondent who watched closely as he wrote it down. In others, people were reluctant to come out of their dwellings and assist in filling out a SIPF. I was advised that one Aboriginal male-only interviewer team had difficulties in eliciting responses from younger women. However, in the cases I observed, I was not aware that this might have arisen because of kinship-based or other restrictions between the person and the interviewer. Rather, it seemed to derive from a strong resistance to being involved in an activity in which the person was totally disinterested. In such instances, the interviewer respected the right of that individual to refuse to participate, in accordance with the importance accorded by Wik to the principle of personal autonomy, and filled in as much of the form as he could himself, with assistance or corroboration from relations on certain questions.

The principal Aboriginal interviewer frequently used humour as a device to circumvent the intrinsically alien nature of the census process. For example, in filling in the form for a young woman classified as his daughter-in-law, and therefore notionally subject to avoidance restrictions, he joked his way through the questions, for example: 'You man or women, eh?', and 'You Island woman eh?'. The use of humour was particularly helpful in eliciting information from children, bringing them and their sharp capacity for observation into the census enterprise. For Wik people at least, this could be construed as 'culturally appropriate' behaviour, since by inverting the usual behavioural codes, the Aboriginal interviewer was also framing the enterprise of collecting the census information as an inversion of normal appropriate behaviour. Implicitly, then, he was also creating a sardonic commentary on the 'silliness' of the census and its questions which was only fully appreciated by Wik people themselves. This particular mechanism would certainly not necessarily be appropriate for other groups, and required an insider's sophisticated knowledge of the bounds of acceptable practice.

Some individuals were provisionally listed as residents of a particular dwelling, but a note was made to check and validate their place of residence at the end of the census collection since they moved between a number of households. This was particularly the case for many children and young men.

Responses to census questions

This section gives brief accounts of some of the issues I observed in relation to specific census questions (see Appendix C for the full forms of the questions on the SIPF).

Question 3

Many people, especially children and teenagers, were not aware of even their approximate ages. Not infrequently, respondents were unsure of the ages of their adult children, of co-resident in-laws, or of actual or classificatory grandchildren living in the household.

Questions 4 and 5

These questions were enormously problematic for Wik people, both in terms of the opaqueness of what it was that was being sought, and in terms of their potential to seriously misrepresent a fundamental set of principles in Wik society (see also extended discussion in Morphy, this volume). One non-Wik interviewer stated that Q. 4 and Q. 5 were 'stupid' and 'offensive'.

The meaning of Q. 5 in particular caused considerable difficulty, including to the interviewers. Some respondents, for example, stated that their closest relation in the house was their child. Others however, ignored closer genealogical relations to nominate a person who had a closer classificatory or other relationship (see immediately below). For Wik people, 'closest' relation refers not just to genealogical distance, but also to the complex combination of that factor and social and political distance.

Often after prompting from the interviewer, people gave their relation to 'person 1' in terms of the simple English equivalent of the Wik kinship term. However, the core conceptual problem is that the kinship system for Wik people provides a fundamental organising principle for their society. Wik kinship terminology is 'classificatory', in the sense that it does not simply refer to close consanguineal kin, but has specific principles by which terms can be extended to classes of people in certain actual or putative relationships. Thus, for example, one's grandfathers and grandmothers are not just the parents of one's actual father and mother, but also include all those persons who are classified in the same generation as one's parents' parents. As another instance, those whom one terms 'father' include not only one's genitor, and possibly also one's mother's husband, but additionally all those whom these individuals classify as 'brothers'.

'Person 1' therefore could have in his or her household more than one mother, a number of cousins, several grandfathers, and a number of sons and daughters who might or might not be their or their spouse's actual children. All these terms would be the English equivalents of particular Wik classificatory kinship terms. Additionally, it could not be assumed that even closely related individuals within the same household shared the same family name; for example, a child could be living with his mother but have taken his father's surname. Conversely, individuals sharing the same surname and living in the same household at the time of the census would not necessarily be from the same nuclear family, although in all likelihood they would be 'family' in the Wik sense.

More broadly, co-residence (even in the limited sense of who sleeps where), commensality, family groupings, and domestic economic units are not necessarily coterminous—for instance, people who live together may not eat together. In common with the situation reported for other Aboriginal groups (Altman 1987; Anderson 1982; Finlayson 1991; Smith 1991, 1992), basic economic and social units of Wik society are comprised of linked households rather than individual ones (Martin 1993). Furthermore, what Aboriginal people themselves refer to as 'families' are typically dispersed across a number of households, as shown in Fig. 2.1 overleaf. This describes a cluster comprising five households drawn from a single 'family' group based on a focal individual and his descendants.

It is clear from the above, and from the observations by Morphy (this volume), that the versions of household relationships recorded on personal forms and which inevitably used English equivalents of Wik kin-based reckoning of relationships could at best offer an impoverished version of the complex maps of social relations with which such traditionally-oriented Aboriginal people operate.

Of course, the census is not designed to reproduce ethnographic realities. However, one can presume that the inclusion of this question in the general census is an attempt to get a broad handle on the changing composition and structures of Australian households over time. The mismatch between the actual complexity of remote Indigenous households such as those in Aurukun, and the impoverished versions that would be recorded on census forms is such as to render the data essentially worthless for this purpose. At most, one could deduce that almost all households involved complex extended family structures.

Fig. 2.1   Example of a 'cluster' of households, Aurukun

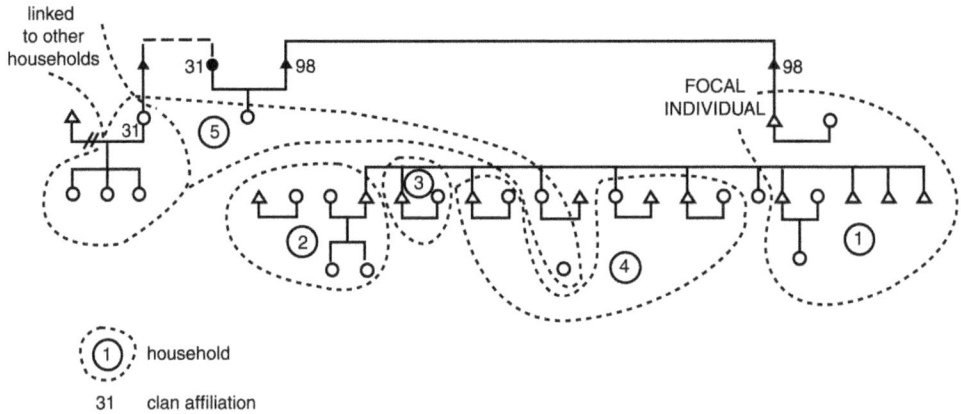

linked
to other
households

31   98

FOCAL
INDIVIDUAL   98

31

5

31

3

2

4

1

(1) household

31   clan affiliation

Source: Martin 1993.

Furthermore, serious concerns must also be asked regarding the validity of the ABS using such data to ascertain family types within households, and the comparability of these findings with those from other sectors of the Australian community. Preliminary results from the 2001 Census provide a breakdown of 'family types' for Aurukun. Table 2.1 provides a summary of the published data, excluding for my purposes here those families where the reference person and/or spouse or partner did not state their Indigenous status. Family types are broken down into couple families with and without children, one-parent families, and other families.

Table 2.1   Family types, Aurukun, 2001 Census

Family type	Families (no.)	Persons (no.)
Couple family	72	389
Couple family with no children	32	80
One parent family	84	351
Other family	6	24

The preceding argument suggests that it is quite invalid to attempt to derive such putative 'family structures' within a particular household, modelled as they are on those of the general Australian society, from the information recorded on the SIHFs and SIPFs. This information comprises for this purpose only the occupants' family names, the English terms for their relationships with 'person 1', and potentially the name of another person in the household to whom they are more closely related, and their relationship to that person. Attempting to cross-validate the nature of the relationship recorded by reference to family names would add no additional rigour, for the reasons outlined above. Such doubts are exacerbated by, but not confined to, issues surrounding the difficulties people had in answering Q. 5 on the SIPF.

Question 6

Responses to this question were treated idiosyncratically by individual respondents. Some with long-term de facto partners stated that they were 'married', while others in the same situation stated that they were 'never married'. At least one person in a long-term relationship refused on principle to have 'married' entered as his status, insisting that if it could not be entered as 'de facto' it had to be entered as 'not married'.

Questions 7, 8, and 9

A series of well-known but nonetheless important issues underlie the difficulties people faced in responding to these questions. Firstly, there is the fact of high mobility rates. People may not be sure where they lived one year ago, or even more five years ago. Phrasing in terms of last 'dry season' as suggested on the SIPF did not necessarily assist. Asking if the dwelling where they are being enumerated is where they live 'most of the time' may not be particularly meaningful for (say a young man) who moves on a frequent basis between households, or even between communities. For many people, it is mobility which is the norm, rather than stability in terms of place of residence—I was asked by a middle-aged man who had visited me in Canberra two months previously if I still lived in the same house!

Related to the above, there is both a high attrition rate and a high construction rate of houses in Aurukun. For many respondents, it was difficult to specify where they lived (say) a year ago, because the house they thought they might have been in no longer existed. While some of the new houses had been erected on sites occupied by now-demolished houses, others were on entirely new sites. While the township streets were named, there was not a conventional lot numbering system. The numbers used on the form were those allotted to houses by the Shire Council, which were not on a street but on a township-wide basis. This made the coding of places of residence one and five years ago even more problematic.

These practical difficulties underlie another issue; it was not clear to the CC or interviewers whether the SIPF aimed to determine only mobility between communities or SLAs, or also that within communities and SLAs. The latter is well demonstrated in ethnographic studies (see discussion above) but whether this is a useful output from a national census may be another question.

I should note here that some difficulties were occasioned by Q. 6 on the SIHF (see Appendix B), regarding from whom the particular house was being rented. All housing stock in Aurukun (apart from government housing for teachers and so forth) is owned by the Aurukun Shire Council. People seemed to idiosyncratically fill in one of the 'community housing group' or 'Government housing authority'.

Questions 10–13

These questions caused problems for interviewers and respondents alike. For a start, my observations of the relatively few Aboriginal people of mixed ancestry in Aurukun were that (for some) Q. 11 and (particularly) Q. 13 caused both embarrassment and bafflement. This is despite the fact that, unlike certain regions in the Northern Territory, to be of mixed descent is not the subject of adverse comment by other Wik Aboriginal people. Rather, the question directly raised (in a semi-public context) the issue of the individual's paternity. Wik interviewer, respondent, and Wik audience, would all have known in each case the imputed paternity of the individual, since such matters are the stuff of everyday gossip and speculation. However, respondents of full descent were not confronted with the same dilemma, whether or not there might be speculation about their actual paternity, since Q. 11 and Q. 13 allowed them to still preserve a general anonymity.

Questions 11 and 12, regarding where the respondent's parents were born, also occasioned diffidence in responses from some, not because they were of particular moment, but because on the contrary the answer was so self-evident. This was but one illustration of an inevitable issue; the necessary question and answer methodology of the census form can result in diffidence, embarrassment, or even hostility for people who, within their own cultural milieu, use quite different means of eliciting information, or of validating information that is already known to be shared. The interviewers often avoided this problem by either prompting the answer for such questions, or simply filling them out without comment.

Question 15

This question clearly caused embarrassment to many if not most respondents. Mostly, interviewers did not even ask this question, or if they did, it was in a clearly rhetorical manner ('You speak English well, eh?'). All interviewers I observed entered either 'well' or 'very well' to this question, even in cases where, to the best of my knowledge, the individuals concerned, young teenagers for example, had quite a limited grasp of English. These observations were borne out in the preliminary census results released for Aurukun and its outstations by the ABS, and shown in Table 2.2 below. These data suggest that the overwhelming majority, some 75 per cent, speak English well or very well, which is not borne out by ethnographic observation.

Table 2.2   Language spoken at home and English proficiency, Aurukun, 2001 Census

Language spoken	English spoken	Persons (no.)
English only		52
Aboriginal language and English:	well or very well	696
	not well	106
	not at all	41
	not stated	4

To make sense of these results, it is important to understand that these responses were not technical in nature but symbolic. As described below, Aurukun had been a church mission until 1978, and the missionaries had placed considerable emphasis on teaching English. As the result of their internalisation of the missionising enterprise within a particular Aboriginal framework, for Wik people of older generations in particular, to be able to speak English well is a sign of being 'civilised', of not being a 'myall'. In arguments, people will disparage others' English capabilities, and conversely boast of their own relations' fluency (Martin 1993). To answer this question with a statement of objective limited capacity, therefore, in a more or less public place (since interviews were almost always conducted outside dwellings with numbers of people present), would have had a powerful negative symbolic import.

Question 16

Aurukun had been a Presbyterian, and later a Uniting Church, mission until 1978. Some (usually) older respondents stated that they were Uniting Church. Many others, especially younger people, stated either that they had no religion, or that they did not wish to answer the question. In fact, the religion question seemed to be largely meaningless to younger respondents. Some interviewers did not provide this option when discussing this question. Not one person that I observed answered 'Traditional Beliefs' to this question, even when interviewers (following discussions with myself) specifically asked this and provided some explanation of what this term might mean. These observations were borne out in the preliminary census results released for Aurukun and its outstations by the ABS. A summary is shown in Table 2.3 below. This data suggests that only a little over 1 per cent of Aurukun's Indigenous population adhere to traditional religious beliefs.

Table 2.3   Religious affiliation, Aurukun, 2001 Census

Affiliation	No.
Uniting Church	171
Other Christian	12
No religion	9
Traditional Aboriginal religion	11
Not stated	715

Yet, Aurukun can still be considered one of the most traditionally oriented communities in Queensland. The Wik people, including those in Aurukun, had only recently had native title over much of their traditional lands recognised, in a process which required extensive documentation of traditional beliefs and practices to be presented to the State government for the purposes of a consent determination. There is a strong system of belief in 'supernatural' forces underlying much of mundane life, including a strong attribution of causality (including through sorcery) which is quite distinct from that of even religious non-Aboriginal Australians (see e.g. McKnight 1981; Martin 1993; Sutton 1978). Why would people therefore resist acknowledging their traditional beliefs?

It could be that one factor is a reluctance to have what lies in the private or internal Aboriginal domain exposed to non-Wik people—but against that argument, Wik people are notoriously outspoken in their views about their cultural distinctiveness. Alternatively, it could be that equating 'Traditional Beliefs' with, for example, 'Uniting Church' in a question about 'religion' is confusing to people. To test this hypothesis, I actually asked this question of respondents myself on two occasions, including using Wik Mungkan, but with no different result.

It could be argued that Aboriginal respondents could see this question in some ways as seeking complementary information to Q. 15 (how well do you speak English). As discussed above, the latter was clearly interpreted by Aboriginal interviewers and respondents alike as being equivalent to asking whether the person was a 'myall' or uncivilised, and it is conceivable that answering Q. 16 in terms of holding 'Traditional Beliefs' would be similarly interpreted, in the context of a census form whose ultimate purpose and destination were quite opaque to almost all Aboriginal people in Aurukun.

In any event, whatever its origin, if this response is broadly consistent with that from other remote Aboriginal groups, one would have to question both the utility of this question (at least as phrased), and also any inferences that might be drawn by subsequent research on the census data concerning the incidence of traditional beliefs amongst remote Aboriginal people.

Questions 19–26

My observations were that if the way in which answers to these questions were given was typical, the census is unlikely to provide a reliable source of data on education and training levels of Aboriginal people in remote communities.

For example, attendance at the Aurukun school has been very low for many years now. Yet, most people that I observed stated in response to Q. 19 that their children went to school, although some rationalised the fact that children were around while the census collection was taking place (during school hours) in terms of such factors as teasing or fighting in the school.

Even for questions concerning post-school courses undertaken, it proved very difficult to elicit clear responses from this cut-and-dried question and answer format. There have been an absolute plethora of training courses which Aurukun people have been involved in over the past few years, and respondents were often vague about the technical details of these courses.

Questions 28–38

Many respondents were not sure of what their before-tax income was. In fact, there is a good argument that Q. 28 (on income) should have followed Q. 29–35. This is would have allowed a logical progression from the general to the particular in the information being sought. Most people are on CDEP, and working from that fact to the number of hours worked would then have allowed the informed interviewer and respondent to jointly estimate the fortnightly income more accurately.

As with dwelling locations, difficulties were encountered in precisely identifying the addresses of people's workplaces; for some CDEP participants, it was entered as 'the yard'. Where interviewers were aware of who worked on CDEP and how many days they worked, the 'hours worked' question was relatively straightforward, since participants worked either two or four seven-hour days. For those on Jobsearch, living in an area where there was virtually no work available, there appeared to be some confusion as how to answer Q. 37 and Q. 38, regarding looking for and availability for work.

Question 39

Census interviewers had a lot of trouble in developing meaningful explanations of this question, and respondents had considerable difficulty in providing meaningful responses to it. In some instances, no attempt was made by the Aboriginal interviewer to provide an explanation, and after an uncomfortable silence, the respondent stated that the information could be kept. Attempts to explain the option in terms of providing a resource for future generations to research family links and so forth made no sense to people at all. For one thing, Wik people hold a deep knowledge of kin links and of the flux of political and social relations—reflected in household compositions at any given time—which is quite independent of any administrative recording of such relations. For another, this question is at the end of the SIPF and follows the manifestly problematic attempts to ascertain information on familial links in Q. 4–6.

Question 40

The format of this item in the SIPF assumes that the interviewer directly interviewed the person named in the form. This was not so in many cases. The interviewer presumably then could have left both Q. 39 and Q. 40 blank. However, interviewers in some of these instances seemed to assume that their signing off the Declaration was not just in relation to Q. 39, but in relation to the information in the form as a whole.

Completion of the count

In the event, the Aurukun census count took almost a month to complete. This was for a range of reasons which were already apparent early in its conduct, including the difficulties in ensuring that as many Indigenous residents as possible were located and recorded, and problems with the availability and commitment to the project of some interviewers.

Conducting the census over such a long period of course has the potential in mobile populations to lead to significant overcounting. Active steps were taken by the Census CC to minimise this. For example, as discussed above, a number of people had travelled to Pormpuraaw for a football match there, and were away for the first week of the census count. The CC checked with a number of these individuals on their return to Aurukun to ensure that they had not been included as visitors in the Pormpuraaw census. Checks were made of a number of individuals who had travelled to Cairns for medical or other reasons to ensure that they had not been included in the census there.

Aurukun's population is characterised by a very high internal mobility (Martin 1993; Martin & Taylor 1996). To minimise the possibility of overcounting because of the extended time taken to conduct the census, the CC prepared a computerised list of all persons recorded on the census forms. Some 40 to 50 individuals, mostly younger children and teenaged boys, were found to have been recorded in more than one household, and duplicates were removed.

As had been planned, spot interviews were undertaken at places such as the store, airport and tavern and outside houses, to ensure that as many people as possible had been recorded in the census. The CC also checked each SIHF and SIPF for completeness of data. The one exception was a mixed household of Indigenous and non-Indigenous residents who insisted on the confidentiality of their forms.

As a final comment on the extreme thoroughness with which the Aurukun census was conducted, the CC was concerned about problems in handling bulky parcels through the mail system from Aurukun to Cairns, and the absence of sufficiently robust packaging, and thus personally delivered the forms to the ABS office in Brisbane.

Conclusion

The conduct of the 2001 census in Aurukun could, from some perspectives, be seen to have been exemplary in terms of its combination of flexibility in a highly challenging environment, systematicity in its collection methodology, and rigour in cross-checking and validating the data collected. Consequently, it is no surprise that the preliminary 2001 census count for Aurukun, at a total Indigenous population of 921, is significantly higher than that from previous census counts; the number of Indigenous residents recorded in the 1996 census was 792. The result would appear to be more commensurate with earlier detailed ethnographic counts (Martin & Taylor 1996).

At the same time, it is clear that the time and human resources committed to the Aurukun census, if repeated elsewhere, would have major implications for the ABS. Were such extended counts to be widespread for the highly mobile Indigenous populations common in remote areas at least, there would be a significant risk of double counting some people, while still missing others. On the other hand, it could be argued that such overcounting would only compensate for the range of other factors which lead to undercounting (Martin & Taylor 1996).

Finally, ethnographic observation of the Aurukun census count, like that in the other case studies in this volume, raises important questions about the rigour and comparability of much of the data recorded on the census forms. It also raises questions about the validity of using census data to derive remote Indigenous population characteristics by means of methodological assumptions appropriate for the general Australian population but not for remote Indigenous people. The ABS have made laudable advances in their Indigenous remote area census methodology, but there is arguably still progress to be made in maximising the capacity of census questions to provide data relevant to central policy issues in Indigenous affairs.

3. When systems collide: the 2001 Census at a Northern Territory outstation

Frances Morphy

Introduction

In August 2001 I observed the conduct of the national Census at an outstation community (henceforth community A), serviced by a homelands association (henceforth HA) which is based at the Aboriginal settlement of B in the Northern Territory. The purposes of this research were twofold: to evaluate the IES as it was applied in this particular context, and to assess the quality of the data that were collected.

This study is being published under terms of the *Census and Statistics Act 1905* Undertaking of Fidelity and Secrecy, which imposes strong principles of confidentiality to protect the anonymity of census respondents. Because community A is small and its residents would be readily identifiable (at least locally) if it were named, the area in which this case study took place is left deliberately vague, and communities are referred to by letters of the alphabet rather than by names. The local Indigenous language is not referred to by name, and where Indigenous language terms occurred in the quotations cited, they are replaced by an English translation in square brackets. The kinship terms of the local system have been replaced by the short-hand forms conventionally used in anthropological publications (see explanation of kinship terminology and abbreviations on p.ix). None of the actors in this story are identified by name: officers of the census are referred to by an acronym for their function, and other individuals are referred to by a letter, or as 'person 1' in a household (where applicable). The dwellings are not individually identified by number. The data on the composition of the study community and of its households are described as if they were actual examples, in order to avoid tortuous syntax, but they should be understood for what they are: artificially constructed data sets that do not correspond to the data on the census forms for the community. The examples are hypothetical, but constructed to bring out the structures and issues that emerged clearly from the actual census data.

The first three major sections of the chapter describe in some detail the recruitment and training of the enumerators and the enumeration process itself. The intention is to provide an ethnographic account of the process in its context, as a background to the main findings and recommendations. Although the IES has been in existence in various forms since the 1976 Census (see Taylor, this volume), there is a dearth of detailed research on its implementation on the ground, and on its effectiveness as a strategy for obtaining complete and accurate information on Australia's Indigenous population.

David Martin and John Taylor, in their observation and analysis of the 1986 and 1991 Census enumerations at the remote community of Aurukun on Cape York Peninsula, found a systematic under-enumeration of children and young adults, and identified several contributing factors, most significantly the mismatch between standard definitions of the 'household' and the 'family' and the facts of Aboriginal social organisation on the ground, and the relatively high mobility of Aboriginal people, both between households and within particular regions (Martin & Taylor 1995: 13, 14–17).

It will be argued in the fourth section that, considered purely as a head count, the enumeration strategy employed at community A in 2001 was largely successful. The reasons for its success are discussed: it is important to understand the reasons for success as well as for failure.

The quality of the data collected is another matter. Particular attention is given, in the fifth part of the chapter, to continuing problems with the definition of 'household' and 'family', and with the questions on the two forms—the SIHF and the SIPF—that compounded the problem of collecting reliable and meaningful data on household structure. In the final section, the quality of the other data is examined.

At a more general level, in these final two sections of the chapter, consideration is given to the kind of information that the ABS is attempting to collect in the census, and whether the design of the forms and of the questions they contain could be better tailored both to the intended respondents and to the goals of the census. The chapter concludes with some general recommendations that flow from the data and the analysis.

The census enumeration in its regional context

The rough estimate for the current Indigenous population of the SLA in which community A is located, derived from the Community Housing and Infrastructure Needs Survey (CHINS) that was conducted immediately prior to the 2001 Census, is 10,000 people.[1] All of this area is remote, and most of its Aboriginal inhabitants are 'traditionally oriented' (to use a convenient shorthand term). The major communities are accessible by reasonable roads in the dry season, but many outstations can be reached only by many kilometres of rough track, or by light aircraft.

The CFO responsible for the enumeration in this SLA planned for a rolling census, with different communities being enumerated at different times, starting in the second half of July and ending by census day itself. This strategy was dictated by the logistics of training the CCs and local Indigenous interviewer-collectors (henceforth enumerators), and processing the results of the enumeration. The schedule was badly disrupted by the deaths and subsequent funerals of two people at two different communities within the SLA. These events delayed or halted the training of the enumerators and the enumeration itself. This was unfortunate for the CFO, for whom it created something of a logistical nightmare.

As will be shown in more detail below, the enumeration in this region was carried out on the basis of persons actually present at a dwelling at the time of the enumeration; that is, according to the standard census procedure. I will argue that if it is consistently administered by enumerators with detailed local knowledge, this strategy is less inherently error-prone and more amenable to verification than the alternative strategy adopted in other areas of the Northern Territory, that of a 'usual residents' count.

The community of A: a snapshot view at census time

The population of community A fluctuates from around 20 (when there is a large ceremony taking place elsewhere) to over 250 (when there is a ceremony taking place at the community); its normally resident population is in the region of 100 people. At the time of the enumeration about 50 per cent of the people listed as 'living here' on the SIHFs were away, at a location where a major funeral that had just taken place, or visiting relatives living elsewhere in the area. But the community was also host to a number of visiting relatives from the immediate region, and from three other communities (C, D and E) outside the immediate region.

The community is structured around the members of two related patrilineages (lineage X and lineage Y) on whose land the community lies. X and Y, the men from whom these two lineages are descended, are classified as brothers. Fig. 3.1 shows the kin relationships, in simplified form, of the people designated as 'person 1' for each occupied dwelling. The census does not capture (because it does not seek to) these inter-household relationships, but it is arguable that the data collected by the census on the composition of individual households make sense only in the context of this larger picture.

Fig. 3.1   Kin relationships between people designated as 'person 1' for each occupied dwelling, community A, Census 2001

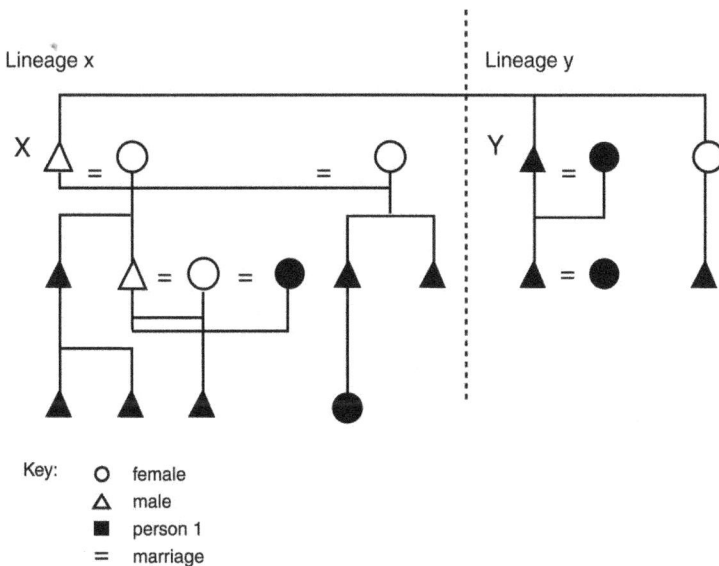

At the time of the census there were 13 occupied dwellings in the community. The census enumeration took place over three days, between 6 and 8 August. During this period the community was preparing for the funeral of an infant who had died the previous week, and it received a visit from a candidate for one of the two major political parties, canvassing for votes in the upcoming Northern Territory election.

Putting the census team in place

For the purposes of the census, the settlement of B and the outstations serviced by the HA are counted as two separate Indigenous Areas (IAs), each with its own CCs. For the HA communities the CFO had appointed two CCs, one local Indigenous and one non-Indigenous, both HA employees. They had different responsibilities: the non-Indigenous CC was in charge of logistics—chartering planes, keeping to the budget, and so on. The Indigenous CC was responsible for overseeing the administration of the census on the ground, and for recruiting and helping in the training of the enumerators. The CFO envisaged his own role as strategic—coordinating the enumeration in the region as a whole, recruiting and training appropriate CCs, and keeping a watching brief on the various stages of the process and the training of the enumerators.

The community census team

At community A there were six enumerators (henceforth E1–6), all but one of whom were residents. The non-resident (E1) was another HA employee who is the son of a sister of X and Y. He acted as the community contact and de facto CC for the exercise. Therefore all the enumerators were well known to other community members, and had detailed knowledge of who lived where, how everyone was related to each other, and of people's present whereabouts.

Fig. 3.2 shows in simplified terms how the enumerators are related to each other and to the apical ancestors (X and Y) of the two major lineages represented at the community. Both E1 and E2 are ZC (sister's children) of X and Y. E2 is the most senior male ZC to the landowning group—a position of some importance in the local social system. E3 is his wife. E2, E4, E5, and E6 are all teachers in the school. E4 and E5 are granddaughters of X, and E6 is one of Y's granddaughters. The significance of these facts will emerge in due course.

Fig. 3.2   The kin connections of the community A enumerators, 2001 Census

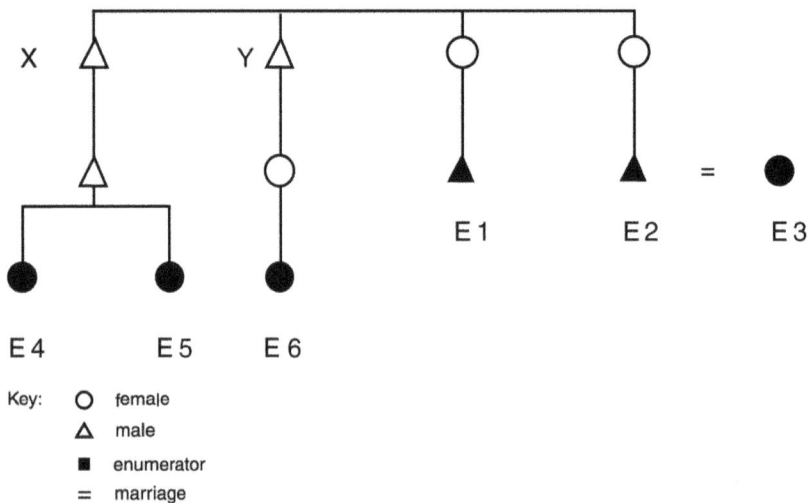

Training

I chanced to meet E1 in the local town centre on Friday 3 August, the day after I had arrived from Canberra. The CFO had already informed him that I was coming to community A to observe the census. He told me that he was one of the enumerators there, that all the enumerators had received their training, and that he was driving down to the community to start the enumeration on Monday (i.e. on the day before census day itself). I surmised therefore that I had missed out on the training and that it had been completed despite the disruption caused by the funerals. It appeared that my only access to information about the training process would be through debriefing the CFO and (if possible) the CCs and enumerators. Accordingly, I arranged to see the CFO on the following day. The account of the training process given below is based on what I learned at that meeting, and on a later meeting with the CFO after the enumeration at community A had been completed.

The CFO told me that the training of the CCs and the compilation of the Dwelling Check Lists for B and the HA outstations had been successfully carried out. The CCs had a map of each community that had to be covered, and a SIHF had been allocated for each occupied dwelling, and each had been given a Census Record Number (RNO). The CCs had been taken through their responsibilities and had been given a set of principles to work to. The Indigenous CC for the HA had been given responsibility for recruiting the enumerators for the HA communities because, the CFO reasoned, he was the person with local knowledge about who could speak to whom and how to get the job done most efficiently. He had suggested that the enumerators be organised to work in teams of two, to avoid problems of people having to speak directly to 'poison' (avoidance) relations.

It was the training of the enumerators that had been disrupted by the funerals. There had been one day of training at community B, in which the enumerators had been shown the training video. It was shown to them all the way through without interruption, in order to give them an overview of the procedure. The emphasis in the training that did occur was on procedure, on ensuring that the enumerators explained properly to the interviewees what the census was, and on the issues of confidentiality and the security of the data. They also spent some time discussing the questions which the CFO predicted would cause difficulties: the questions on kinship (on the SIHF, and Q. 4 and Q. 5 on the SIPF—see Appendices B and C), and Q. 39 on the SIPF, which asks whether the respondent agrees to having their name and address and other information from their form kept in the National Archives and then made publicly available after 99 years.

The CFO was doubtful that the kinship questions would yield useful data, because he was aware that local Indigenous kinship terms and English terms are different. The enumerators were instructed use to English kinship terms first, and to use local terms only in cases where clarification was needed. The CFO went through the basic English kin terms to ensure that the enumerators knew the meaning of terms such as *niece, nephew, uncle* and *aunt* as well as of the more core kinship terms of the English (henceforth Anglo-Celtic) system.

The CFO spent some time with the enumerators on Q. 39, explaining its meaning and getting them to practice asking each other the question and to devise a local-language version to use during the enumeration. His main concern was that the taboo on the use of the names of dead people would lead people to answer 'no' to the question, so the emphasis given was to the forms being locked away in Canberra for a considerable period of time.

Because of the interruption to their training, the enumerators had not had the opportunity to familiarise themselves with the forms in detail, nor to practise going through them. On the Monday the CFO was planning to go to community A with the Indigenous CC and E1 to finish the training. His intention was to let the CC and E1 conduct the training; he would intervene only as necessary, if something had been missed or clarification of some point was needed.

From training to doing

I arrived at community A on the morning of Monday 6 August in advance of the census party, and went to the school, where the other enumerators were gathering. The CFO, the CC and E1 arrived shortly thereafter by vehicle. Everyone was there except E2, who came about half an hour later.

The session proceeded. It quickly transpired that the enumerators were going directly to filling out the SIHFs, apportioning them between themselves as they went. The CFO and I noticed this separately, more or less simultaneously. He decided to allow further training to proceed 'on the job'. He continued to observe what the enumerators were doing, and intervened with instructions if he saw something not being done correctly, or if he was asked directly for advice. The CC and E1 were also advising the other enumerators.

Household members and visitors were listed from memory on each SIHF in turn, and also absent members of households (who were marked 'no' for a SIPF). These lists were not inviolate: later on, as the enumerators went round the houses and discovered in more detail who was there and who was away, the yes/no column was changed, as people were added or subtracted.

The CFO instructed explicitly that the family name should go on the top of the SIHF, then the head of the household should be listed as person 1. This person, he suggested, would usually be the father, then the mother and rest of family should follow. He reminded the enumerators that for every person the second name had to be filled in as well as the first.

The CFO also instructed explicitly about where the RNO and dwelling number should go (the enumerators were not filling those in until he told them to). The enumerators went to the map to find the dwelling number (the lot number), and then cross-referenced to the Dwelling Check List to find the assigned RNO. I was having trouble with this system, but it appeared to cause no difficulty to the enumerators.

The SIHF also asks for the age of each person and their relationship to person 1. The enumerators used the school roll for the ages of the children (and the teachers), but everybody else's age was a guesstimate. E1 had compiled a list of everyone's ages derived from local clinic records, but he had left it behind at the HA office in community B. He commented that this did not matter, because the ages could be fixed up at the office later.

There was some discussion about how to translate local kin terms into their English 'equivalents'; this topic was to recur throughout the enumeration. 'Wife', 'husband', 'son', and 'daughter' were unproblematic: everyone was familiar with how these are applied, even though they do not correspond to local terms. E1 reiterated that English terms had to be used, not local terms. The question of kinship and how it was reflected on the SIHFs and SIPFs is discussed in some detail below.

E1 explained that a SIPF was needed for everyone on the SIHF who was present at the time of the enumeration. 'Even the little children?' he was asked, to which he replied in the affirmative.

There was considerable discussion about how to treat visitors and absent residents: both the enumerators and the CFO were aware of the complex possibilities. E4 asked what to do about visitors from other communities. The CFO said visitors should be included on the SIHF of the dwelling at which they were staying, and marked as 'V'. They should be asked if they had been counted anywhere else, and that if not they should have a SIPF filled out. In cases of doubt it was better to be on the safe side and do a SIPF, otherwise they might be missed altogether. One of the women expressed shyness about asking visitors for their details.

The CFO was also asked: 'How can you ask questions if someone is not here?' The questioner had in mind someone who was away on a trip, and who would be staying in a hotel. The CFO said that anyone like that would be counted at the hotel on census night, so they should go on the SIHF, but should not have a SIPF done for them. More generally, anyone who was away in a place where they would be counted should not get a SIPF. He was asked: What about people who are away at community C or D? The CFO suggested doing SIPFs just in case they got missed there. What about people who would be coming in tomorrow for the funeral of the baby? The CFO suggested doing a SIPF if they had not been counted anywhere else and if the dwelling was still in the process of being enumerated. But if the enumeration of the house had been completed they should not be added.

E1 suddenly remembered the tent in the front yard of one dwelling. It was normally occupied by the mother-in-law and father-in-law of 'person 1' at that dwelling, who were on an extended visit. They were away at community B, but had left initially to attend a funeral ceremony elsewhere. The CFO's view was that since the tent was not a permanent dwelling, and its usual residents were in any case visitors to the community, it should not be registered, and so it had no SIHF, and no SIPFs were attached to it. Its absent residents were not included as visitors on the SIHF for the dwelling.

After all the household forms had been completed, the CFO suggested counting the number of SIPFs needed for each dwelling and putting them in an envelope with the SIHF. E1 and the CFO both stressed several times that the SIPFs had to be filled in at the house wherever possible.

During this process at least one extra person was remembered for one house. There was some further discussion about people who were currently down as 'yes' but who turned out not to be there. The CFO suggested that if they did not come back during the process of enumeration they should be changed to 'no', and that no SIPFs should be done for them. At this point, one dwelling was listed as a vacant dwelling because all the occupants were away. However they returned during the process of enumeration, so the status of the dwelling was changed and SIPFs were done for the returned occupants.

The households were initially divided up between the enumerators as follows:

- E2 and E3 took the forms for their own dwelling and for three of the dwellings occupied by descendants of X;

- E1 and E6 took the forms for the other four houses occupied by descendants of Y (including their own dwellings, or, in E1's case the dwelling he was 'visiting' at);

- E4 and E5 took the forms for the other four houses occupied by descendants of X (including their own dwellings).

Thus the workload was distributed fairly evenly, and everyone except E2 and E3 was assigned to their own 'side' of the community. E2, the most senior ZC to the apical ancestors of the two lineages, was assigned dwellings from both sides. One of the dwellings assigned to him turned out to be the most problematic in terms of the enumeration, because it contained some visitors from community E who were not all that concerned with—indeed who actively evaded—being counted.[2]

As far as I am aware, the final page of the SIHF (number of bedrooms, number of vehicles, etc.) was not filled in at this session, and I do not know when these details were added. I assume that the characteristics of the dwellings could have been added later from HA housing records, and the enumerators would have had a good idea of how many vehicles there were in the community and who owned them.

E1, in his decision to get everyone to complete the SIHFs at this session, was operating on the assumption that the training of the enumerators had been completed at B earlier. In a sense this assumption rested on a minor failure of communication between him and the CFO. The CFO later told me that the 'training' session described above was a unique occurrence: the enumeration had not proceeded at any other community in quite this way. When they set off to begin the enumeration, the enumerators had still not gone through the SIPF in detail, or familiarised themselves with the questions.

However, E1 was operating on another, correct, assumption: that he and his fellow enumerators knew their community well enough to fill in the SIHFs before proceeding to the enumeration proper. In doing so, they spared the interviewees a lengthy part of the process entailed in following the 'proper procedure' (see Will Sanders, this volume). The filling in of the SIHFs at this point turned out to be an advantage rather than a disadvantage: this point will be revisited below.

The session was indeed a training session in some respects. At the end of it, the CFO could be confident that the SIPFs would be correctly identified, and properly cross-referenced to their SIHFs. Between them, the CFO and the enumerators established a clear set of procedures for dealing with absent residents and visitors: the enumerators were alert to the possible permutations and the CFO held to a clear set of principles, based on the standard enumeration procedure, which he applied consistently to these permutations. They also had discussions that were as useful as they could be (which is to say not very) on the translation of kin terms.

The enumeration proceeds

I was able to observe parts of the enumeration directly at ten dwellings (one visit each to nine dwellings, and two to the remaining dwelling). Only three of these visits were complete enumerations, because at every other house visited there were some people off hunting (or away from the dwelling for other reasons) and the enumerators followed the strategy wherever possible of returning to households to catch people rather than filling out the SIPFs in their absence. They also filled in SIPFs for people who they found at someone else's dwelling (if they had not already been enumerated), and later filed them with the correct SIHF.

Day one

On the afternoon following the filling in of the SIHFs, I went with E1 and E6, who made their initial visits to three dwellings. They also went briefly to E2 and E3's dwelling and helped them to fill in the SIPFs for their own household. We finished in the early evening. The CFO and CC had stayed on for part of the afternoon, and the CFO dropped in on each of the three pairs of enumerators to check on progress and to field queries. Of the dwellings visited on this day, only one was completely enumerated.

The interviews on the first day took longer than on subsequent days. The enumerators were familiarising themselves with the SIPF as they went, and in the process were trying to work out what some of the questions meant.[3] They also began to devise standard replies to some questions.

Day two

The following day (census day itself) I went back with E1 to one of the dwellings we had visited the previous day. E1's aim was to complete the SIPFs for this dwelling, which had 22 people on the SIHF: six residents who were actually there, 10 absent residents, and six visitors from community D. We had missed the visitors and several 'usual residents' on the previous day, because they were out fishing, but we got there early enough to catch them this time. E1 was assisted once more by E6, who lives in that dwelling. E1, E6 and I then went to the last dwelling on their list to conduct the enumeration there. By the time we finished there it was lunchtime.

In the meantime, the other enumerators had made their initial enumerations in all but three of the dwellings designated to them. After lunch everyone except E2 met back at the school 'office', where the envelopes were being deposited as the forms were completed. E1 was already in the role of chief enumerator for the lineage Y side of the community. During this session E4 began to assume the equivalent role for the lineage X side of the community, and they continued in these roles for the rest of the enumeration exercise. Working together, E1 and E4:

- checked that the SIHFs and SIPFs were in their correct envelopes (some were not);

- checked the SIHFs against their completed SIPFs to determine who had not yet been 'caught';

- double-checked against the school register to make sure that all preschool and school-age children resident in the community had been covered;

- amended the SIHFs in the light of their now up-to-date information about absent and newly present residents and visitors;

- assigned SIPFs for people who had been missed so far (including the entire household of the dwelling which had previously been classified as vacant, and one as yet unenumerated dwelling);

- apportioned the remaining work.

E1 also began the task of making the responses to certain questions on the SIPFs consistent. For example, all schoolchildren and preschoolers were put down as speaking English 'not well'. E1 commented to me after the enumeration was complete that they had been learning how to fill in the SIPF during the process of enumeration. He was aware that as a result the answers to certain questions were not filled in consistently across the whole enumeration, and he did his best to remedy this after the fact, during this and a later checking session.

Following the checking session I went with E1 and E4 to a dwelling that had been on E4 and E5's original list, but which they had not had time to get to the day before. E1 and E4 managed to complete the enumeration of the dwelling in a single session, and they also persuaded one of the community E visitors (who was on the SIHF of another dwelling, but was sitting with his brother at this dwelling at the time) to fill in his SIPF. It was later added to the appropriate envelope. We then moved to the dwelling that had been listed as vacant on the previous day, and a complete enumeration of its returned occupants was successfully achieved. It was now evening again, so work stopped for the day.

Day three

The day began with an announcement over the community megaphone that one of the local candidates in the upcoming Northern Territory election was coming that morning to canvass the community. People were urged to attend, and were keen to do so, and the enumerators were anxious to complete their task beforehand. E1 and E2 were heavily involved in preparations for this visit, and so three of the female enumerators (E4, E5, and E6), with me in tow, went as a group to continue the mopping up of the remaining 'missing persons'.

We proceeded first to a dwelling where some of the occupants had not yet been enumerated. Person 1 and his wife were the parents of the infant who had recently died, and whose funeral was shortly to take place, so the enumerators were reluctant to press anyone who was not feeling like being questioned. In addition, person 1's wife and her sisters are from community C. People from community A and its region characterise women from there as excessively shy and retiring, and this proved to be the case.

While we were at this house we saw the community E visitors departing in their vehicle from the dwelling which was to be our next port of call. We went there nevertheless, and one additional person was enumerated. He had returned from community B on the eve of census day. Our final visit was to a dwelling where the 'person 1' had not been enumerated, and there we also found his father, who was an as yet unenumerated 'person 1' for another dwelling. They had their SIPFs filled in rather hastily because the plane bearing the local candidate had just landed, and both men were anxious to get to the meeting.

The enumerators had been continuing to return the finished forms in their envelopes to the school 'office'. Most of the envelopes were there by this time. E4 and I now went there, and E4 began a second cross-checking session. Once the local candidate had departed we were joined by E1. E4 began by checking the SIHFs against the SIPFs once again. She noticed that one of the community D visitors had been enumerated twice at two different dwellings, and eliminated one of the forms. She also noticed that two community C visitors had still evaded enumeration, and marked them down for chasing. We already knew that all but one of the community E visitors had escaped being enumerated, but at least they were on the SIHF for the dwelling where they had been staying.

The envelope for that dwelling had now been returned, and it was discovered at this point that none of the SIPFs for the dwelling had in fact been fully filled in. The envelope for the dwelling was marked 'not complete', and it was subsequently visited again by E4 and E1.

As each SIHF and its attached SIPFs were checked, E1 and E4 filled in missing details on any partially completed forms that they found, including those for the community E visitors. They only filled in information that they were reasonably certain of. They were also checking for incorrectly filled forms (for example if people who were pensioners had also been put down as being in work). As each SIHF and its SIPFs were completed, they were placed in their envelope and it was marked as 'complete'. At this stage they did not fill in the summary on the second page of the SIHF. This was presumably done back at community B, when E1 went through the forms with the CFO.

My systematic observation of the enumeration ceased at this point. I have described the process in some detail in order to convey the context in which the enumerators were operating and their strategies for achieving the best possible result, as they perceived it, in the circumstances.

The enumeration: a preliminary evaluation

There is no doubt that the majority of the enumerators had taken on board the training that they had been given, were concerned to do the job well, and applied considerable ingenuity, flexibility and dedication to their task. It could also be said that, as far as enumeration scenarios in Indigenous communities go, this was a good one. This was a discrete small-scale community, and the ratio of enumerators to dwellings was almost 1 to 2. Moreover, the enumerators knew the community (and the comings and goings of its members) extremely well. Most of the people they were interviewing were close kin, and willing to cooperate.

There were, however, possible instances of double counting and of omission. These will be discussed in a later section. It is notable, too, that it took six enumerators over two days to enumerate the inhabitants of 13 dwellings. The reasons for this will become clear in the discussion of the interviews that follows.

The interviews

While the enumerators were filling in the SIHFs before the enumeration proper, E1 remarked to me: 'It's a bit rude in [the local Indigenous] way of thinking to ask these [white people's] questions. We have to be careful about asking them.' He was to reiterate this sentiment more that once during the enumeration, and it clearly influenced the conduct of the interviews. The second major influence was the sheer size of the SIPF, and the time that it took to administer. Many of the strategies adopted could be interpreted as streamlining devices.

Conducting the interviews

During the day, most people sit outside when they are at home, so the enumerators simply walked up to each dwelling and announced to the assembled company that they were here to fill in the census. Most people already knew what they were doing, and very few raised any kind of objection, or asked for further information about the census. People who evinced shyness or reluctance (these were mainly youths or young adults of both sexes) were cajoled by their assembled relatives into cooperating. Here, the fact that the enumerators were well known to everyone worked to their advantage, and to the advantage of the enumeration process. People largely took it on trust that the census was a good thing, and saw their cooperation in personalised terms: they were helping their enumerator kin to do their job properly.

Everybody found the process of the interview a bit strange: they were Indigenous actors in a non-Indigenous scenario. Although everyone would normally speak to one another in the local language, the enumerators initially asked the questions in English, and the respondents replied likewise. However, if the meaning of a question was unclear, or the answer not straightforward, people usually switched to the local language for the ensuing discussion. The enumerators were asking kinds of questions that local people rarely ask one another, either because both parties already know the answer (name, sex, kinship relationships, marriage status, place of residence, origin and ancestry), or because they are about matters that are not of central concern (age, level of education, source of income, nature of paid work, hours worked). Humour was the main device used by both the enumerators and the interviewees to reduce the awkwardness of the occasion. There were many jocular false answers, and jokes at the expense of white people for wanting to know these things.

On the first day, E1 and E6 quickly settled into a standardised routine, that varied only slightly according to circumstance. Each person at the dwelling who was on the SIHF was asked to come and sit in turn with the enumerators. E1 asked the questions, while E6 filled in the form. In general, E1 also supplied the answers, verbally, to the questions for which he thought he knew the answers, and on occasion the interviewee would correct him, or a discussion would ensue before the question was finally answered. He directly questioned the interviewee only when he was uncertain of the answer.

Once everyone who was present had been interviewed, the household in general was asked about those who were absent. If a person was somewhere in the general area, but not actually at home, they were kept as candidates for SIPFs and noted down (mentally) for a later visit. In some cases it was discovered that people who had been marked as 'no' on the SIHF, because the enumerators had thought they were away, were in fact in the community. Their status was changed to 'yes' on the SIHF, and if they were actually present their SIPF was done. If a person who had been marked as 'yes' was actually away (at community B for example), their status on the SIHF was changed to 'no'. Significantly, the enumerators did not ask if there was anyone else who *should* be on the SIHF, and no one at the dwellings volunteered extra names, at least not in the cases I observed. Thus, if the enumerators had missed off any 'usual residents' when they compiled the SIHFs, the chances were that those people would be missed, unless they were actually present at the time of the interviews.

If there was anyone present at a dwelling who was on the SIHF of another dwelling, the enumerators also took the opportunity to do a SIPF for them, if they had not already been interviewed, on the principle of 'a bird in the hand'. This was a potential source of error: SIPFs could have got into the wrong envelopes, and the possibility of double counting also arose. Such errors did occasionally occur, but, as we have seen, they were picked up and corrected during the checking sessions at the school.

The interviewers were clearly committed to completing every SIPF in the presence of the interviewee. But had they asked everyone to respond to each question, the sessions would have dragged on interminably. In most cases their solution to this problem speeded up the interviews while not seriously compromising the quality of the data. E1 had a clear idea about which questions required answers from the interviewees and which questions he knew the answers to. Because the forms were filled out in the presence of the interviewee, that person had the opportunity to correct E1 if he got something wrong. That certain categories of people were less likely to do so was a possible source of bias: men and senior women were more likely to interject than were children and young women. Every interview took place within earshot of other household members, and there were often interjections from them in such cases.[4] It could be argued, then, that the SIPFs of young women and children reflected less of their own knowledge about themselves and more of the opinions of the enumerator and more senior family members.

Adapting to circumstance

The general atmosphere of cooperation was weakened or broke down with two kinds of respondents: visitors from other communities and women from community C families, whether they were visitors or 'usual residents'. Although all visitors were kin to someone in the community, they did not necessarily know the enumerators very well. The community D visitors were cooperative when 'caught', but elusive: hunting and fishing were much higher on their list of priorities than filling in the census. The community E visitors, as we have seen, showed no desire to cooperate: the one who was 'caught' at his brother's house at first tried to evade the process ('We're only passing through, we don't live here'), but eventually gave in to pressure from the enumerators and his brother's family.

For the community C women, especially the younger ones, the whole process was just too culturally inappropriate. They refused to answer out loud, retreated physically into the dwelling, or refused to come out to be interviewed. The enumerators adapted their interview strategy accordingly. Only female enumerators attempted to conduct these interviews, and they took place inside the house, or off to one side, in lowered voices. When all else failed the forms for the women were filled in later by the enumerators on the basis of their knowledge of the individuals concerned.

Other circumstances sometimes forced variations on the theme. One of E1's MMBD (the sister of his actual MMBD, or 'mother-in-law') lives at one dwelling. In local society a FZDC ('son-in-law') and the women he calls MMBD, whether actual or classificatory, must avoid physical proximity and eye contact, and may only converse indirectly through an intermediary. The fact of working in pairs, as the CFO had correctly predicted, rendered this unproblematic. The CFO was also correct in his estimation that it was best to leave the handling of such situations to the enumerators themselves: avoidance behaviour is an everyday part of local life, and there are strategies already in place to accommodate it. It is not uncommon for a MMBD and her male FZDC to be members of the same household, since elderly mothers often live with one of their daughters. E1's MMBD simply sat where she was. E1 had positioned himself at some distance from her and out of her direct line of sight, and E6 had sat down between the two of them. Interestingly, E1 and E6 still maintained their roles. E1 asked the questions in a quiet voice. E6 relayed the question to E1's MMBD, E1 then answered the question (or the MMBD provided the answer herself), the answer was relayed by E6, and then E6 wrote the answer down if there was no dissent from either of the other two parties. E1 was unable to ask Q. 2 and Q. 4–6 (the questions on sex, kinship, and marriage), because a FZDC may not speak about, or hear anyone else speak about such matters in regard to his MMBD. E6 asked these questions herself, in a whisper, or simply wrote the answer down without asking. When it came to Q. 39, E1 tried to get E6 to ask it, but she was hesitant. So he asked the question quietly and she then repeated it word for word to the MMBD.

Although the enumerators tried always to do one SIPF at a time, there were times when they departed (or were forced to depart) from this principle. In the case of small children, where it was a parent or another relative who was helping with the SIPF, the enumerators often took one form each and worked on them simultaneously. This was not because children were considered less important, but rather because the enumerators quickly realised that filling in a form for a person under 15 years of age was more straightforward since several questions did not apply to them.

At two of the dwellings I visited, the enumerators were compelled to fill in more than one adult form at a time, or even to hand over the SIPF to the interviewee and allow them to fill it in for themselves. This was because the interviewees were about to go off hunting or fishing, and were anxious to be on their way. In one case the interviewees were some of the community D visitors, and in the other they were a group of local young men. The enumerators judged (almost certainly correctly), that people would vote with their feet if the interview process took too long, and so they resorted to this procedure. These SIPFs were subsequently reviewed during the checking sessions, and in some cases added to or amended in the light of the enumerators' personal knowledge of the interviewees.

I now consider briefly the responses to each of the questions on the SIPF, roughly in the order in which they appear on the form. The full versions of the questions on the form are found in Appendix C.

Basic details (Q. 1–3)

Because the SIHFs had been filled in previously, the interview always began at Q. 1 of the SIPF. The enumerators did not follow the instruction to copy the answers to Q. 1–4 from the SIHF, but instead used Q. 1 and Q. 2 as a joking introduction. It is noteworthy that Q. 1, Q. 3, and Q. 4 are posed as direct questions on the form, which seems to contradict the instruction at the top of the form, but another factor that might have been significant here is that the enumerators considered it no more peculiar to ask these questions than any of the others.[5]

In Q. 1 (What is your name?), people's first names were sometimes spelled differently from how they appeared on the SIHF. One or two people appear under one name on the SIHF, and another on the SIPF. Everyone has several names, and the name by which they are referred to can change over time, for example on the death of someone who shares the name that is in current use. In one or two cases, interviewees said that their 'registered' name should be put on the SIPF, even if it was not the name they were currently addressed by.

Real difficulties began at Q. 3 (How old are you?): almost no one knew how old they were. Where they did know their year of birth they calculated their age with reference only to the year, not their actual date of birth.[6] Quite often, the age recorded on the SIPF was different from the guesstimate that had been entered by the enumerators on the SIHF.

Kinship (Q. 4 and Q. 5)

The responses to Q. 4 (How are you related to Person 1 (Head of house)?) will be discussed in detail in a later section. The enumerators tried very hard to follow instructions, used English kinship terms themselves, and encouraged the interviewees to do so as well. The results will be uninterpretable. Q. 5 (Are you more closely related to anyone else in the house?) was quickly abandoned, at least in the interviews that I observed, for reasons that will become clear.

Marriage (Q. 6)

The question (Are you married?) posed no problems to the enumerators or the interviewees.[7] However the data collected at community A may cause some puzzlement to the sharp-eyed analyst. Two dwellings contain a female person 1 who describes herself as married, but no evidence of a cohabiting spouse in either case. Why do these women describe themselves as married, rather than as widowed, separated or divorced? The reason is that local Indigenous marriages are often polygamous: it is not at all uncommon for a man to have more than one wife (and often those wives are sisters). It has become common nowadays for a man to live with only one of his wives, and for the other wives to occupy one or more separate dwellings. In local terms this does not constitute either separation or divorce, if the relationship between the two parties remains amicable. In both the cases mentioned here, the husband lived in a nearby dwelling with another of his wives.

Residence (Q. 7–9)

The 'place' questions also caused few problems for the enumerators and the interviewees, but the data almost certainly do not reflect what the census was after. 'Place', which is not further defined, was interpreted to mean 'community' rather than 'dwelling'. Moreover, people identify closely with the community as their home, even though they are at times highly mobile, and a 'yes' answer to Q. 7 (Do you live at this place most of the time?) reflects that identity rather than a computation about which community the person actually lives at 'most of the time'.

The instruction to give a street number, street name, suburb, and postcode if the answer to Q. 7 was 'no', as in the case of visitors, caused some hilarity. No one thinks in these terms. Although the community does have street names they are never used as a point of reference. Mail is not delivered house to house in this community. It does not have a street directory. People think in terms of 'X's house', or 'the new house', or 'the blue house' (see Musharbash 2001: 4 for similar observations about Yuendumu). This is generally true of all communities in the region, even the larger settlements.

The ambiguity of the word 'place' did surface with respect to visitors, because the dwelling at which they were enumerated tended to be the 'place' at which they usually stayed when visiting the community. The use of the verb 'live' (as opposed to 'stay') was not enough of a trigger to automatically generate the correct response. However, after discussion, the meaning of place as 'community' took precedence, and the home communities of visitors were put down as their usual place of residence. Little attempt was made to think seriously about where anyone was actually living one and five years ago (Q. 8 and Q. 9). The default assumption was that the answer was the same as Q. 7, that is the community with which the person identifies.

This group of questions was invariably answered hastily and in a formulaic way, for three reasons. One derives from local Indigenous culture, in which place has very different connotations from those it has in the mainstream, and in which years, as a unit of measurement, have little significance. The two other reasons concern the design of the SIPF questionnaire. Because the questionnaire took so long to administer, the enumerators tended to supply, or readily accept formulaic answers to, questions that appeared to have self-evident answers, or which appeared, in local terms, to be unimportant, or even absurd. For this particular group of questions this impulse was compounded by the design of the questions themselves. There is something very offputting about being asked to provide a complete address, three times in a row, when one's dwelling does not have that kind of address, or, even if it does, is never thought of in those terms.

Origin and ancestry (Q. 10–13)

These questions appeared at first sight to cause no problems at this community, where everyone is unambiguously of Aboriginal 'origin' (Q. 10) and 'ancestry' (Q. 13). A distinction between the two was also discerned—but it is not the distinction that the questions are aiming for. The details of the small print in Q. 13 (What is your ancestry?) draw on an implicit distinction between 'Indigenous', 'ethnic' and 'unmarked' (that is, Anglo-Celtic). These are not 'natural' categorisations, but ones embedded in the culture of mainstream Australia. Local Indigenous people do not categorise people in the same way. Moreover the content of these two questions is very problematic: neither says explicitly what information is really being sought.

I take Q. 10 to be a question concerning cultural identity (although it is not expressed overtly as such), and Q. 13 to be a question about biological (or 'ethnic' origins). The presence of the word 'ancestry' in Q. 13 led local people to a different interpretation. Ancestry was glossed by the enumerators as [sacred ancestral inheritance].[8] Thus Q. 10 was interpreted more as an enquiry about ethnic origins (or biology pure and simple) and Q. 13 as a more complex enquiry about spiritual (or cultural plus biological) identity and origins. The 'right' responses were obtained, but for the wrong reasons.

The small print in Q. 13, which provided a clue as to the intent of the question, was noticed and often read out by the enumerators, and jokes were made about people's ancestry. The tendency to treat the small print as a joke in this question was encouraged by the examples given for possible ancestries (Vietnamese, Hmong, Dutch, Kurdish, Australian South Sea Islander, Maori, Lebanese). Most are improbable ancestries for local people of mixed descent. Because of this the examples given were not sufficient to override the interpretation of 'ancestry' as [sacred ancestral inheritance].

Q. 11 and Q. 12 (Was your father/mother born in Australia?) were generally treated humorously, because the answer to both was so self-evidently 'yes' in all cases.

Language (Q. 14 and Q. 15)

The responses to Q. 14 (Do you speak an Aboriginal or Torres Strait Islander language at home?) were an accurate reflection of reality, in that everyone said they spoke an Aboriginal language at home. This is certainly true. For people who were from other linguistic regions, the 'language' name given tended to be a general one, and to correspond to what a linguist would classify as a language.

For local language speakers (the majority in this community), a much more complex picture emerged. The local Indigenous language is a language in the linguistic sense: it is a group of mutually intelligible dialects. But local people (and this includes the enumerators) rarely use the term that has been coined to designate the language. They commonly distinguish 'language' at two levels. They distinguish groups of dialects on the basis of their forms for the word 'this', and/or distinguish 'language' at the level of landowning group. Sometimes the labels are used separately, sometimes together. To the uninitiated, the census data would thus indicate that many different 'languages' are spoken in this community, whereas in reality most of the 'languages' identified are variants of one single language. Moreover, the *same* variant may be recorded under three different labels: 'this', 'landowning group' or 'this + landowning group'.

Q. 15 (How well do you speak English?) was answered with a high degree of accuracy, although there was some debate about whether the phrase [a little bit, somewhat] should be translated as 'well' or 'not well'. People are in general able to assess objectively their level of competence in English.[9] Adults tended to assess their own level of competence, and the enumerators accepted their self-assessment. For children, however, the enumerators adopted a formulaic approach: infants and pre-school children were said to speak English 'not at all', and schoolchildren were said to speak it 'not well', 'because they're just learning'. In one case a man wanted to put that his small grandson spoke English well, but he was overruled by the enumerators.

Religion (Q. 16)

Q. 16 (What is your religion?) generated much debate; people wanted to mark more than one box. Many if not most local people are 'bi-religious'. As one interviewee put it: 'My beliefs are traditional, but my religion is [Christian denomination]'. The reasons for this lie partly in the mission history of the region, for by and large the founders of the missions in this area were respectful of the local religious belief system and did not attempt its wholesale repression, and partly in the nature of the local Indigenous metaphysic, which is incorporating and syncretic rather than exclusive. One might say that for local people their traditional religion is their Old Testament, and Christianity is their New Testament. Each has its place and function in the contemporary worldview.

There is no explicit indication that it is permissible to mark two boxes for this question. E1's solution was to mark only 'Traditional Beliefs', often declaring as he did so, '[Indigenous] comes before [white man], so we'll put Traditional Beliefs'. Most interviewees agreed to this. The other enumerators sometimes marked both [Christian denomination] and 'Traditional Beliefs', and sometimes only one or the other, depending presumably on what the interviewee's response was.

Computers and the Internet (Q. 17 and Q. 18)

There are no computers in the community, so not surprisingly everyone responded 'no' to these questions. This is not to say that no one knows how to use a computer. At least one person put a computer course down at Q. 23, and the teachers and HA employees in the community all use computers to some degree in their work. The base school at community B makes use of the Internet, and the community teachers may well have some experience of using it.

Education (Q. 19–22)

Q. 19 (Do you go to school, TAFE or university?) and Q. 20 (What type of school or place of education do you go to?) caused no problems, and were answered accurately. One person was in the middle of a teacher-training course of some kind, but it was difficult to decide which box to mark in Q. 20 because it was an in-house course at the homelands school headquarters in community B.

Q. 21 (Are you 15 years of age or more?) was found to be odd, because people had already said their age earlier. The enumerators finally recognised it for what it is—a cue to go to the end of the questionnaire if the interviewee is under 15 years of age.

Nearly everyone had difficulty with Q. 22 (What is the highest level of primary or secondary school you have completed?), including those enumerators who are teachers. The prompt 'Year 8 or below' had no salience for them: had the term 'primary' been used there would have been no problem. Very few local people have more than primary education, and the outstation school has no post-primary section. Even most of the teachers went no further within the school system as such. For those people who had been educated in 'mission time' this question was even more difficult to answer, and it was sometimes left blank.

Further education (Q. 23–27)

The vast majority of interviewees answered 'no' to Q. 23 (Have you *finished* a trade certificate/apprenticeship, TAFE course or university course since leaving school?). For those few who answered yes, the box that was always marked was 'Yes, other course'. This was a *faut de mieux* response, because people did not know whether the courses they had attended were or were not a 'trade certificate/apprenticeship'. Q. 24 (What is the name of that course?) caused some problems because what is really being asked for is the name of the qualification rather than of the course, but the wording is misleading. Most of the courses people had done were not certificate, degree or diploma courses. Under 'Full name of course' people invariably put a descriptive title rather the name of the qualification, so that the information supplied there tended to overlap with or be the same as that supplied for Q. 25 (What did you study?). Q. 26 (What was the name of the place you studied at?) caused difficulty for some because their courses had not taken place at a particular institution. For Q. 27 (In which year did you *finish* that course?), most people were able to produce the certificate that showed when the course finished.

Money each fortnight (Q. 28)

HA policy is that people without other regular sources of income (e.g. pensions, or 'real' jobs) who live at outstations are paid for 20 hours of CDEP work per week. This was the case for the majority of adults in community A. For these people, the amount recorded at Q. 28 (How much money do you get each *fortnight* before tax?) was always the same, that is $320–$399 per fortnight. The enumerator rather than the interviewee supplied the answer. If people were on a pension of some kind, the enumerator also filled in the amount. I did not ask the enumerators how they knew the correct answers to this question: clearly they had either been instructed on the right figures to enter, or had thought to find them out prior to the enumeration.[10]

No attempt was made to compute other sources of income, for example from art production or royalties, although several members of the community derive income from one or both.

I suspect that this is because, in comparison to the known income from CDEP and pensions, the enumerators felt it would be too hard to elicit this information. Income from these other sources does not come in a steady stream, and it would have been very difficult to work out a fortnightly amount. The subject was never raised, either by the enumerators or by the interviewees.

Did you have a paid job *last week*? (Q. 29)

For people on CDEP, the answers given to this question were correct—but for the wrong reason. The question was interpreted as 'Did you have *a pay* last week?' Fortunately, the previous week had in fact been a CDEP pay week. This question needs to be rephrased if it is to be asked next time. The word 'worked' or 'work' needs to find its way into the large print in the main question.[11] The local interpretation of the question suggests that for local people, as far as CDEP is concerned, the word 'pay' is more salient than the word 'job'.

Job description and content (Q. 30 and Q. 31)

Q. 30 (What job did you do *last week*?) and Q. 31 (What things did you do in that job *last week*?) caused difficulties initially until the enumerators worked out what the difference was. A standardised response emerged: Q. 30 was answered with 'community service' and Q. 31 with what the actual 'work' consisted of. 'Jobs' included 'community leader' and 'home management', and there were a lot of 'rubbish collectors'. The enumerators and interviewees were clearly responding to the prompt in the question, which lists only 'jobs' that would be considered as such in mainstream terms. No-one put down 'making art works', or 'hunting' or 'fishing', although many people on CDEP spend more time in those kinds of activities than in those contained in the prompt to the question. For example, after discussion with the enumerators, one person answered Q. 30 with 'community work', and Q. 31 with 'community leader'. His brother from community E remarked: 'you should put artist'—an entirely reasonable suggestion since person 1 is one of the best known artists from the region, whose works are found in national and international collections. The suggestion was not taken up.

Who is the employer? (Q. 32–34)

The wording of Q. 32 (Who did you work for *last week*?) focused people on the local community, rather than on the HA which administers the CDEP program. The word 'for' in this question has more than one possible interpretation. It can mean *for whose benefit* did you work? Or alternatively it can mean 'who did you work *for in your capacity as an employee*? The use of 'who' forces the first interpretation: the community, which consists of a collection of known individuals, is a more salient candidate for 'who' than is an organisation based at community B. The small print did not help in this case, because the word 'community' cued the name of the community rather than the over-arching organisation.

Q. 33 (What is your workplace address?) caused the same difficulty as other questions that asked for addresses. There are only three official 'workplaces' in the community— the school, the community shop, and the clinic (which did not function on a regular basis at the time). Like dwellings, these workplaces are not thought of in terms of their address. These questions were clearly not formulated with remote communities in mind.

Q. 34 (What work does your employer do?) focused people's attention on the HA, because of the presence of the distancing word 'employer'. People do not regard their own community in those terms. The counter-intuitive instruction in small print to write 'community council' was overlooked, except by one community D visitor. Instead, the enumerators devised a formula to describe the activities of the HA (variations on 'provides community programs').

Hours of work (Q. 35)

The answers provided to this question (How many hours did you work last week?) were formulaic. If a person was on 20 hours of CDEP the answer was '20'; if they were in full-time CDEP the answer was '40'. The enumerators supplied the answer, and no one disagreed. No attempt was made to compute the actual number of hours worked, and it would not have been possible to do so: nobody wears a watch or keeps track of time by the hour in the outstation context.

How do you get to work? (Q. 36)

This question provided another opportunity for humorous responses, because everyone gets to work on foot. Levity was not unwelcome at this stage in the proceedings!

Looking for work (Q. 37 and Q. 38)

Q. 37 (Did you look for work at any time in the *last four weeks*?) and Q. 38 (If you had found a job, could you have started work *last week*?) were both answered in the negative by everybody, including those on CDEP. A common comment by the latter in reply to Q. 38 was 'no, because already got a job'. By this stage the interviewees had clearly realised that CDEP was being treated on the SIPF as payment for 'work', and were happy to fall in with this definition.

Consent (Q. 39) and Declaration (Q. 40)

The enumerators had been carefully schooled to ask Q. 39 (see Appendix C) in the local language; they had evolved a formula for it during their training session and had practiced asking each other. The CFO's concern, transmitted to them, was about people being uneasy about hearing the names of dead people. The question as asked in the local language focused on the form being put away in a safe place in Canberra for a long time, and being brought out [when you are a old person, so that you or your grandchildren can see it, and see your name there]. The period of 99 years was interpreted as [a long time], but the precise period of time was not really understood. Put in this way, consent caused no problems for local people, who recycle names from grandparent to grandchild: 'it's OK, because your [(Z)DC] will be using that name by then'. Everyone answered 'yes', but it is arguable that they were responding to a different question from that actually being asked in Q. 39.

Q. 40 asks for the interviewer to declare that they have explained the requirements of Q. 39 to the person interviewed, and that they have correctly recorded the person's views at Q. 39. However, the interviewers did not at first read the small print, and the early forms were signed by the interviewee, at the request of the interviewer. E1 noticed the small print at some point during the first day, and thereafter the interviewers signed the forms.

A complete enumeration?

Two overarching factors—the legendary mobility of Aboriginal people coupled with the logistical necessity of the rolling census under the present arrangements for enumerating Indigenous populations in remote regions—militate against the achievement of a 'perfect' enumeration. In terms of coverage, the enumeration at community A was as good as it could be: as far as I could ascertain, there was no systematic under-counting or double counting in the community itself. There were isolated cases of each, and these will be discussed below because they may point to potentially systematic sources of error. However, it was not possible to gather systematic data on the enumeration (or non-enumeration) of absent 'usual residents', and it is possible that, as noted earlier, up to 50 per cent of 'usual residents' were not in the community during the enumeration.

The success of the enumeration flowed from several sources. The community is relatively small and its 'usual residents' have a strong sense of belonging to it. There was little difficulty in defining who counted as a 'usual resident', whether absent or present, and who was a 'visitor', although local definitions of these terms do not coincide absolutely with those envisaged by the designers of the census (this point is discussed further below). The local knowledge of the enumerators, who were well and appropriately recruited, was also a very significant factor, in two ways. Their detailed knowledge of the community ensured that coverage was as complete as humanly possible, and their membership of the community, as kin to the interviewees, ensured the community's cooperation (on the whole). Finally, the training that the enumerators received, although curtailed, was quite evidently effective. They knew in principle what they had to achieve, and had been given the necessary tools to carry out the task successfully.

The 'ceremony effect'

At one dwelling the SIHF listed 12 'usual residents', five of whom had been at community B staying with a relative at the time of the enumeration there. They were listed on the SIHF of that relative's dwelling as visitors, and enumerated at community B.[12] These people were still at community B when community A was enumerated, and so did not have SIPFs done at community A. A sixth 'usual resident' of the dwelling (person 10) had gone to community B to join the other five, and then left for a funeral ceremony elsewhere before the enumeration at community B. He was, nevertheless, enumerated at community B in absentia, because he was expected to return there to join his other 'visitor' relatives. However, he returned directly to community A and was enumerated there, as a 'usual resident'. He was not asked if he had been enumerated elsewhere, but even if he had been asked he would not have known that he had already been counted at community B with the other five 'visitors' from community A.

Although this was an isolated case of double counting, it resulted from factors endemic to the context of the enumeration of the region. Other cases of the kind almost certainly occurred. The funeral mentioned above attracted many people from the region, who were then, of course, absent from their usual places of residence—or from the place where they were recognised as 'visitors'—for the duration. It would have been quite inappropriate to conduct the enumeration during the ceremony, and so this was not attempted: the community where it took place was enumerated after the ceremony was over. The enumeration at community B occurred while the ceremony was on, and anyone who was known to be at the ceremony, who would normally have been at community B (as a resident or as a visitor), was enumerated at there 'as if' they were there. Thus anyone who, like person 10, subsequently left the ceremony and went to an as yet unenumerated outstation instead of returning to community B was a potential candidate for double counting. There appears to be no perfect solution to this conundrum. Had the people attending the ceremony not been enumerated in absentia, those who returned to community B would not have been enumerated at all, because the count at community B had been completed before the ceremony ended.

Funeral ceremonies are, alas, all too common in the region. During the two months I spent at community A in 2001 there were two funerals in the community itself. Preparations for two other major funerals at nearby outstations were under way when I left. Funerals and other types of ceremony are a major cause of unpredictable short-term population mobility in the region: some people are almost continuously on the move from one ceremony to another, and some ceremonies attract large numbers of people for short periods from across the region. No dwelling-based enumeration strategy can ever be devised that will fully counteract the effects of this specific type of intra-regional mobility, because it would never be appropriate to conduct the census enumeration at a community during a ceremony. The practice of enumerating ceremonial attendees as if they were in their usual place of residence is a departure from the principle of enumeration in situ, but it is better than failing to enumerate them at all.

The effect of other kinds of short-term mobility

Person 1 from a particular dwelling in community A was at community A when the settlement B enumeration took place. However, she subsequently went to settlement B for a short visit, and was still there when community A was enumerated. She was therefore not enumerated either at community A or at settlement B. Note, however, that although no SIPF was done for her she did appear as person 1 on the SIHF for her dwelling at community A.

I suspect that this was not the only case of this kind in the region, despite the best efforts of the CFO and the CCs and enumerators. The residents of an entire dwelling at community A would have fallen through this same crack had they not serendipitously returned to the community while the enumeration was in progress. Cases of double counting (other than ones of the 'ceremony effect' type detailed above), where someone happened to be present for the enumeration in two different places at two different times, might also have occurred, but this is less likely because 'visitors' were usually asked if they had already been enumerated elsewhere. However, at community A at least, 'usual residents' were not asked if they had been enumerated elsewhere as a visitor.

Assessing the extent of under-enumeration and double counting

It would be possible, in theory, to assess the extent of under-enumeration and double counting by comparing the SIHFs for the whole region (i.e. settlement B and its associated outstations), looking for people who were listed as 'usual residents' but were absent, and then searching to see if they appear as enumerated 'visitors' at some other community. It would also be possible to check whether 'visitors' in one place had also been counted at the place where they were 'usual residents'. But this could not be done efficiently without the help of the local enumerators. They alone would be able to narrow down the range of possible alternative locations for such individuals: people's short-term movements are never random, but are constrained by considerations of kinship and attachment to place. People might also be under different names on different SIHFs, or their name might be spelled differently. Again, only someone with local knowledge would be able to make correct cross-identifications in such cases.

It is important to note, however, that this type of cross-checking is only possible if:

- every dwelling in a region, including those which are temporarily vacant, has a SIHF on which all usual residents are listed, and on which all visitors present at the time of the enumeration are also listed;

- 'usual residents' are listed as either present or absent, and only have SIPFs filled out if they are present;

- all visitors who are listed on the SIHF also have a completed SIPF; and

- exceptions to the above are clearly defined and adhered to. Usual residents who are absent at the time of enumeration, but will not be enumerated in the place where they are, for example at a ceremony (or at a sports carnival—see Martin and Sanders, this volume), should be enumerated 'as if' they were present.

The count at community A approached this ideal, as did the count at settlement B and in the region generally.

A 'usual residence' count, where everyone was enumerated on a SIPF according to their usual place of residence, whether or not they were actually there at the time of the enumeration, would be an alternative, but less satisfactory, strategy. The quality of the data on the SIPFs would suffer, since many more SIPFs would be filled out in the absence of the individual concerned. Moreover, visitors who were actually present would not be enumerated, on the assumption that they were being enumerated at their usual residence, in absentia (see Sanders, this volume). Such a strategy is therefore also much more dependent on the robustness of the definition of 'usual resident'.

The worst-case scenario would be one where these two strategies were mixed within a single region. This would result in a high incidence of both double counting and under-counting, and it would be well nigh impossible to cross-check the data.

The role of the SIHF

Whichever strategy is adopted, the SIHF is a crucial tool. Because it lists both absent usual residents and visitors, it provides a snapshot of the level of inter-community mobility, and it provides a means of checking for double counting and under-counting. However its usefulness is dependent upon two definitions: that of the 'dwelling' and that of 'usual resident'.

In small cohesive communities such as community A, the definition of 'usual resident' is unproblematic, although the local definition does not correspond to the ABS definition. For one thing, as we have seen, it is the community rather than the particular dwelling within it that people have in mind as the 'place' where they reside. The ABS definition of 'usual resident' is also based in the notion of calendar time, and this does not apply to the local definition, at least not in such an absolute sense.[13] For example, some of the absent 'usual residents' of one dwelling at community A had been at community B more or less continuously for over a year, because one of their number was doing a year-long course at the local Health Centre. Nevertheless these people consider themselves, and are considered by others (including the enumerators at both A and B) to be 'usual residents' of community A and 'visitors' at community B, because community A is the locus of their most significant personal and spiritual attachments, and is the place they intend to live in the long term.

However, even within this region, and more so in other areas of Australia, the notion of 'usual resident' has been, and most probably continues to be, problematic. If the census is viewed strictly as a snapshot view, the data contained on the SIHFs accurately reflect the general situation: Indigenous people are highly mobile, and at any one time many will be 'visitors' at places other than their 'usual residence'. But it would be unwise to use the census data as the starting point for a more fine-grained analysis of attachment to place and patterns of mobility.

What constitutes a dwelling?

The case of the absent tent-dwellers from the yard of one dwelling highlights the other definitional problem alluded to above. These people were, for the moment, 'visitors' at community A, on an extended visit to their daughter, but happened to be absent (at community B) at the time of the enumeration at community A. Because their tent was a 'non-house' with no occupants who were usual residents of the community it was not designated as a vacant dwelling, and so it had no SIHF. Nor was it counted as part of dwelling that it was pitched next to. It is highly unlikely that these people were enumerated on SIPFs elsewhere. It is also possible that they did not appear on a SIHF anywhere. They have a permanent dwelling at another outstation, but that dwelling was currently vacant.

At the time of the enumeration, this happened to be the only tent in the community, but had the enumeration taken place in the following week, there would have been several more. Many 'usual residents' had returned by that time, and most houses in the community are too small to house their full complement of inhabitants comfortably. Until recently people got round this by sleeping on the veranda (if there was one), or out in the open. But tents have become very popular locally over the last two or three years, and are easily obtainable at affordable prices in the local town. They are now regularly used as extra bedrooms if a house becomes overcrowded—either temporarily (as when visitors arrive for ceremonies) or in the medium term, when the full complement of usual residents is present.

Functionally, these tents are extensions of a permanent dwelling, and their occupants are, more often than not, 'usual residents' of the dwelling and members of the dwelling's household. The difference is only in the eye of the non-Indigenous beholder, for whom a tent is a 'temporary dwelling' rather than an 'extra bedroom'.[14]

Missing persons 1

Had I not been present, a significant number of 'person 1s' at the community would not have been enumerated on a SIPF. According to the CFO this did not happen anywhere else in the region, but it is worthy of discussion because it highlights a particularly salient point of difference between local Indigenous and mainstream social structure and cultural values. I did not notice the systematic omission immediately, because the first two dwellings we visited on the first day did not result in complete enumerations. At the third dwelling, however, I noticed that no SIPF was completed for person 1, in this case the oldest member of the community.

I asked the enumerators if they were going to do a SIPF for this man, thinking that they had just overlooked it because he was inside the house. To my surprise, they said that they did not think it was needed. I decided at this point that I would be doing everyone a favour if I temporarily abandoned my 'observer' status. (And besides I was intrigued: what could the reason be?) So I asked why. The answer was that it was not necessary for person 1 in each household to have a SIPF done, *because their kinship relationship to everyone else in the household was already specified on the SIHF.* Thus at this stage they were thinking of the SIHF as person 1's SIPF.

What led them to this conclusion? The reasons must have been powerful, for they produced what might be called a culturally induced 'blind spot': they overrode the principles which had been inculcated during training—principles which the enumerators had obviously otherwise taken on board. And indeed it took more than one conversation to convince them that SIPFs were needed for these individuals.

There were several factors that conspired to produce this 'mistake'. Question 4 on the SIPF asks for information that has already been recorded on the SIHF. So indeed do Q. 1, Q. 2, and Q. 3—but with an important difference. For local people, the most salient question on the entire SIPF is Q. 4, because kinship is the central organising principle of their society. The misapprehension that person 1 does not need a SIPF is reinforced by the design of Q. 4 (see Appendix C). It asks in big bold letters how the person is related to person 1. The little box for marking if the person *is* person 1 needed to have explicit instructions beside it, in lettering the same size as the main question.

For the enumerators, Q. 4 simply did not apply to person 1. This fact overrode all else, and their view was reinforced by the design of the SIPF. If Q. 4 had been placed further down the SIPF, it would not have acted as a brake to further questioning of person 1; placing Q. 4 in such a prominent position carried the implication that the information it elicited was as significant to the author of the form (i.e. the ABS) as it is to local people, which is to say that, by comparison, the other information elicited by the SIPF is relatively unimportant.

As will be evident from the general thrust of this paper, the advantages of employing local enumerators in Indigenous communities far outweigh the disadvantages, and no criticism of the enumerators is implied here. But Indigenous enumerators are being asked to do something very difficult, to deploy the skills and knowledge that they have acquired as members of their community, while simultaneously assuming the position of temporary 'outsiders'—agents of the state as it were. The designers of the SIPF need to be more aware of this delicate balance. Kinship is not as important in the 'mainstream' society as it is for Indigenous people. It is certainly not so important that it renders other information irrelevant. If questions on family relationships are to be asked, they should be in a less prominent place; or they should be radically rethought. This issue receives further discussion in the next section.

The 'household' and its structure

Questions 4 and 5 on the SIPF attempt to elicit information about household structure using the idiom of kinship. All socialised human beings—including those raised in societies where the Anglo-Celtic system prevails—view their kinship system and its kinship terms as 'natural', because they are inculcated at such an early age. However, the kinship terminology of mainstream Anglo-Celtic Australia, like local Indigenous kinship terminology, forms an elaborate abstract system in which terms only have meaning in relation to the overall structure of the system. If two kinship systems differ markedly in their structure, it is not possible to simply translate the terms from one system to the other. The principles according to which the Anglo-Celtic system is constructed differ markedly from the principles underlying the local system. In the following discussion I hope to show conclusively that it is impossible to elicit information about one such system in terms of another, and that the data resulting from such an attempt are doomed to be uninterpretable.

Kin terms: a comparison

In the Anglo-Celtic system, the term *cousin* is used to refer to the children of a person's (ego's) father's sisters and brothers, and of their mother's sisters and brothers. In other words, the system merges under the term *cousin* all the children of ego's parent's siblings. Note also that the Anglo-Celtic term *cousin* is neutral with respect to sex. Anglo-Celts call the children of their own father and mother either *brother* or *sister*, depending on their sex. The local Indigenous system is completely different. Local people call the children of their mother's brother MBC and the children of their father's sister by a different term, FZC. A MBC may also simultaneously be a MMBDC, and the same term is applied to both categories of relative. Like *cousin*, these terms are neutral with respect to sex. Put another way, the system distinguishes two kinds of cross-cousins: matrilateral (MBC) and patrilateral (FZC). Local people call the children of their mother and her sisters and of their father and his brothers B if they are male and Z if they are female. In other words, in the local system siblings and parallel cousins are merged. Like the Anglo-Celtic terms for siblings, these too are differentiated by sex. Fig. 3.3 illustrates the differences between the two systems for the set of terms for siblings and cross and parallel cousins.

Fig. 3.3   Siblings and cousins in the Anglo-Celtic and local Indigenous systems

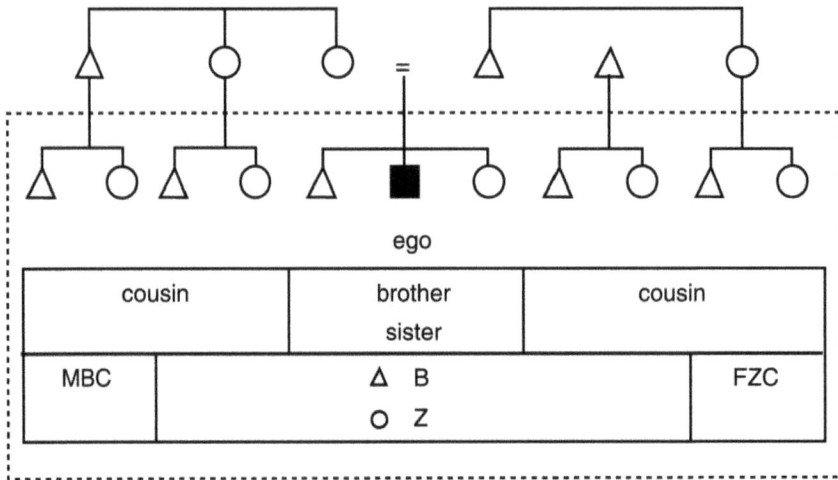

People raised in the Anglo-Celtic system think of *son* and *daughter* as 'natural' categories. Children are defined, as it were, with respect to their parents' marriage: both parents use the same terms for their offspring. The children of ego's brothers and sisters are merged under the term *nephew* for males and *niece* for females. The local Indigenous system operates according to a different set of principles, which appear just as 'natural' to local people. A woman calls her own children and those of her sisters ZC, and those of her brothers by a different term, BC. A man calls his own children and those of his brothers BC, and those of his sisters ZC. Children are here being defined not with respect to their parents' marriage, but with respect to their lineage: BC means 'child of my patriline' and ZC means 'child of my matriline'. These terms for children (as with Anglo-Celtic *cousin*), are not differentiated according to sex. Fig. 3.4 illustrates the differences between these sets of terms in the two systems.

Fig. 3.4   Children in the Anglo-Celtic and local Indigenous systems

Male ego

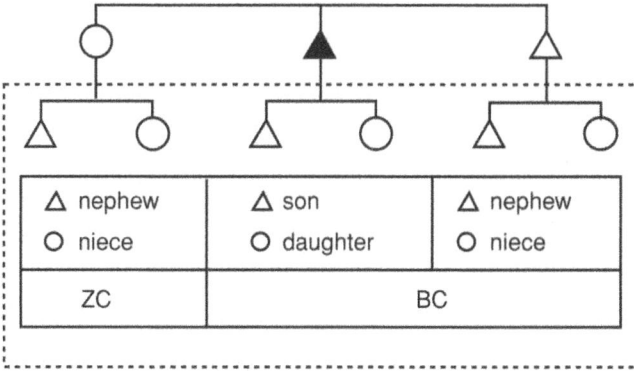

△ nephew ○ niece	△ son ○ daughter	△ nephew ○ niece
ZC	BC	

Female ego

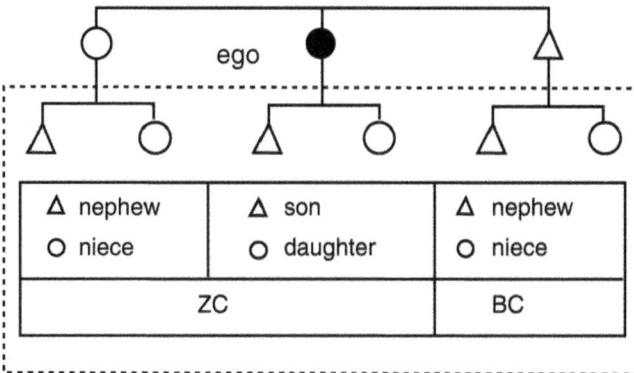

△ nephew ○ niece	△ son ○ daughter	△ nephew ○ niece
ZC		BC

All kinship systems have terms that are 'classificatory' in the sense that they classify people together according to a set of underlying structural principles. The term *cousin* is probably the most classificatory of the Anglo-Celtic kinship terms (although *uncle, aunt, grandparent,* and the category *in-law* are quite complex as well). But the local Indigenous system applies more (and more abstract) principles of classification than does the Anglo-Celtic system. For example, males in the generation above ego in ego's patriline (including ego's own father) are F, and all females in the generation above ego in ego's mother's patriline (including ego's own mother) are M. But these terms have even wider application: they apply also to kin in generations other than the parental generation.

Fig. 3.5   The Anglo-Celtic term *mother* and the local Indigenous term M compared

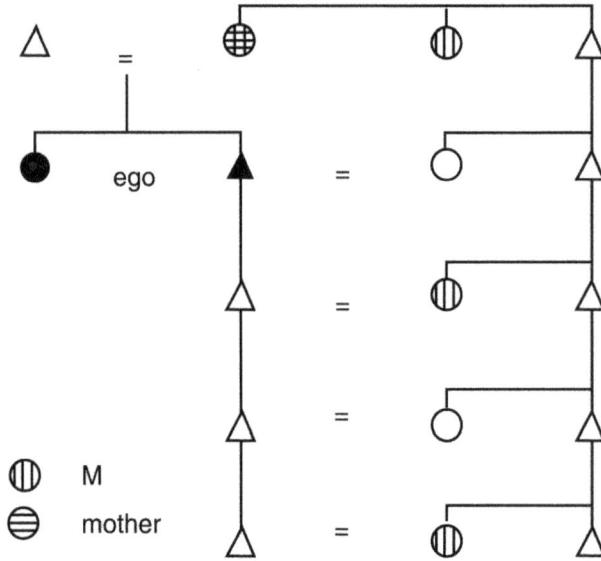

If one thinks of ego's own generation and the generations of their grandparents and grandchildren as 'even' and ego's children's, parents' and great grandchildren's generations as 'odd', the term M applies to any female member of ego's mother's patriline who is in an 'odd' descending generation with respect to ego (see Fig. 3.5). No M is any more or less of an M than any other, just as no *cousin* is any more or less of a *cousin* in the Anglo-Celtic system.[15] People have been told that M means 'mother', and so that is how M was often translated by the enumerators, whether the person was, in Anglo-Celtic terms, a *mother*, a *daughter-in-law*, a *nephew's wife*, a *great granddaughter-in law*, or a *brother's great granddaughter-in-law*. The last two, significantly, are scarcely kin terms at all in the Anglo-Celtic system. Sometimes the enumerators, realising that some categories of M do not count as *mother* in the Anglo-Celtic system, attempted to substitute the 'correct' Anglo-Celtic term—with varying degrees of success, as we shall see in the case of one dwelling (see Fig. 3.7 and the accompanying discussion). None of the Anglo-Celtic terms for the kin comprising the 'nuclear family' are directly translatable into local Indigenous kinship terms. And vice versa: none of the core terms, let alone the non-core terms, of the local Indigenous system are directly translatable into Anglo-Celtic kinship terms. The Anglo-Celtic reader, who is probably suffering from 'kinship fatigue' at this point, should bear in mind the plight of the Indigenous enumerator, who is faced with exactly the same problem (seen from the other side), in a real-time interviewing situation.

The local Indigenous and Anglo-Celtic systems differ in another very important way. In the Anglo-Celtic system (as it operates today), people are rarely kin to one another before they get married. A marriage brings together, in a set of *in-law* relationships, two previously unrelated kindreds. Their only point of intersection is the married couple—the *husband* and *wife*—and the connection is then carried down into the couple's descendants.

In the local Indigenous system, the preferred marriage is between people who are already in a kinship relationship: a man marries his (actual or classificatory) matrilateral cross-cousin: his MBD. A woman thus marries her (actual or classificatory) FZS. Marriage in the Indigenous system does not *create* bonds of kinship: it reinforces and reaffirms *already existing* kin relationships. So a man's MBD may be his wife, but she is also a kind of *cousin* in the Anglo-Celtic system, and a man's male ZC (actual or classificatory sister's son) is his *nephew* in Anglo-Celtic terms, but may also in addition be his daughter's husband, or *son-in-law*. Thus it is perfectly possible for a woman with no daughters and an unmarried man to refer to each other as FZDC 'son-in-law' and MMBD 'mother-in-law' respectively, as happened on one SIHF and the related SIPFs.

The Indigenous kinship terminology encompasses categories of people on which the Anglo-Celtic system is silent. It distinguishes and covers seven patrilines that are related matrilineally through the marriage system. The Anglo-Celtic kinship terminology focuses on the individual and their direct ancestors and descendants, and merges patrilineal and matrilineal kin at every level. The system fades off very quickly into *cousins* and then non-kin as soon as it leaves the realm of ego's nuclear families of origin and procreation. In the Anglo-Celtic system there is no term for (Z)DDFZC, who is the person (or the sister of the person) who potentially marries your (Z)DD (daughters' daughter from a female point of view, and sister's daughter's daughter from a male point of view). E1 and I had several conversations about how such a person should be characterised in English. The option of classifying a (Z)DDFZC as a 'friend', or as 'unrelated', did not enter the frame.

For Q. 4 the enumerators were often successful in assigning the 'correct' term—in Anglo-Celtic terms—with core kin. In at least one case, a father's brother, who in local terms is another F ('father') was put down as 'uncle', and the use of the terms 'nephew' and 'niece' corresponded to Anglo-Celtic usage. The enumerators' own superficial knowledge of the Anglo-Celtic system and the training provided by the CFO thus had some effect. But it did not penetrate very far into the system.

It should now be clear that in the context of local Indigenous kinship, Q. 5 is unanswerable. Even if one is operating according to the Anglo-Celtic kinship system it is difficult to know how one might answer it. Who is closer to ego: father or mother? In a three-generation household, who is closer to ego: parent or child? Is the relationship to a spouse closer than to a child? Is the relationship to a sibling closer that to a child? What precisely is meant by 'closely related'? Is it a question about biology, or a question based on unexamined assumptions about what constitutes closeness in terms of a particular system of kinship? It is not surprising that this question was left blank on the majority of SIPFs. E1 commented at one point: 'this is a real [white man's] question', by which he meant that it made no sense in local Indigenous terms.

Household composition

Anglo-Celtic kinship, then, is not the ideal idiom for attempting to elucidate the structure of local Indigenous households. But what of the implicit model of the household that lies behind the census questions? The definition of the household given in the *2001 Census Dictionary* (ABS 2001) allows for the possibility of more than one 'household' in a dwelling, but not for households whose membership is spread across more than one dwelling. Two major types of 'household' are identified: those whose members are 'related' (family-based households), and those whose members are 'unrelated' (group households).

In the ABS definition of the family, 'the basis of a family is formed by identifying the presence of either a couple relationship, lone parent-child relationship, or other blood relationship ... *other related individuals* (brothers, sisters, aunts, uncles) may be present in the household' (ABS 2001; emphasis added). Although the ABS does not use the term 'nuclear family' it is clear from the definition that this is what is meant by a 'family', since other 'related individuals' may be associated with it, but are not part of it. Daly and Smith provide a succinct account of how the ABS categorise the data obtained from 'multi-family' households: '[T]he nuclear family of parents and children is taken as the base around which all family types are constructed, and other families within the household are placed in relation to this "primary" family ... if there are more than three family types in a household, the adults in any additional families are "disbanded" as a family type, reclassified as related individuals, and assigned to the "primary" family' (2000: 12).

The model does not fit the Indigenous facts on the ground. Indigenous households 'who make common provision for food or other essentials' (ABS 2001) are often spread across more than one dwelling (for example in the case of a man and his co-wives, as discussed elsewhere in this paper). Moreover, previous ethnographic work on Indigenous household structures led Daly and Smith to conclude that: 'the nuclear family is not the most common residential form ... indigenous households in the 1990s were characterised by considerable compositional complexity, porous social boundaries and large size' (1999: 2). These generalisations continue to hold true for the households at community A in 2001.

Table 3.1 shows the 'usual residents' of dwelling J as they were listed on the SIHF for the dwelling. The local Indigenous kinship term by which person 1 actually addresses each person is given in the last column. Superficially, this looks like a four generation family, consisting of person 1 and his wife, their daughter and her husband (who is also person 1's sister's son, and hence *nephew*), two of the daughter's children, and person 1's wife's mother. A perfectly 'normal' pair of related nuclear families, plus one mother-in-law, one might think, although the fact that person 1's wife and his daughter appear to be the same age gives grounds for suspicion that all is not as it seems on the surface.

And indeed it is not, as Fig. 3.6 shows. Person 2 is indeed person 1's current wife (and also, as it happens, his actual MMBDD), and person 3 is indeed her mother. But person 4 is the daughter of person 1 and his deceased first wife, and the two 'grandchildren' far from being person 4's children, are people who would not even be classified as kin in the Anglo-Celtic system. They are the great grandchildren of person 1's mother-in-law's deceased husband's other wife. In the local Indigenous system, these children are considered kin to person 1. Their mother is his classificatory BC ('daughter'). He looked after her when she was a child, and now her children live in his household.

Table 3.1   Details of dwelling J as recorded on the SIHF, 2001 Census

Person no.	Age	Relationship to person 1	Indigenous term
1.	56		
2.	34	wife	MBD
3.	70	mother-in-law	MMBD
4.	34	daughter	BC
5.	38	nephew	ZC
6.	5	grandson	BDC
7.	10	granddaughter	BDC

Fig. 3.6   Dwelling J: actual relationships of usual residents

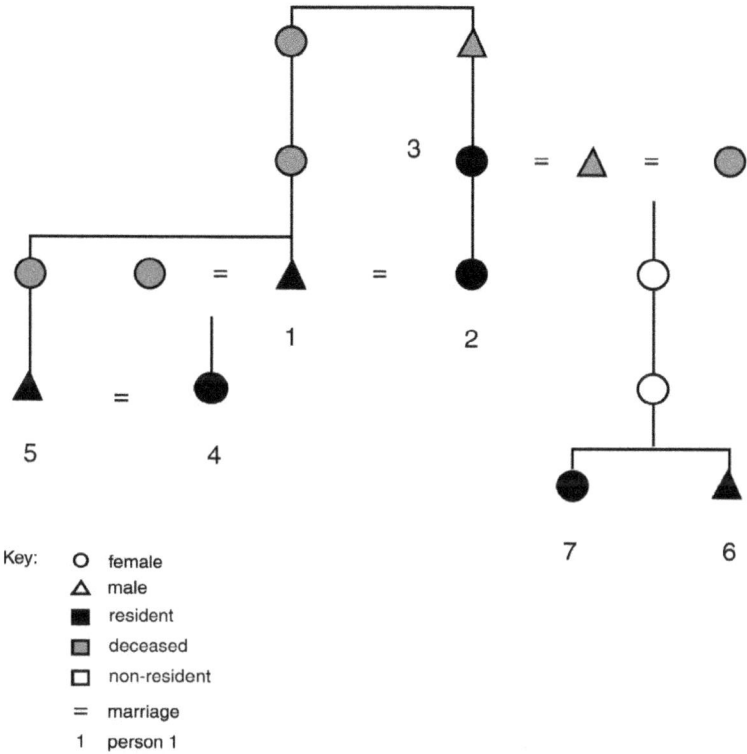

Key: ○ female
        △ male
        ■ resident
        ▨ deceased
        □ non-resident
        = marriage
        1 person 1

Another possible scenario in cases where a dwelling contains people who are kin in the Indigenous system, but not according to the Anglo-Celtic system, is demonstrated by the case of dwelling K. A partial genealogy for this dwelling is given in Fig. 3.7. This dwelling had 11 'usual residents'. In one case the Anglo-Celtic kin term entered in response to Q. 4 differed from the one entered on the SIHF: person 5v (a woman) was put down as 'uncle' on the SIPF and as 'daughter' on the SIHF. Person 10 (an 8-year-old boy) was put down as 'sister's son-in-law'. Person 8 was put down as 'brother-in-law' and his wife, person 9, as 'granddaughter'. Person 6 was put down as 'great-granddaughter'. In terms of the kinship diagram, and the Anglo-Celtic system, these responses seem to be not only wrong, but also incomprehensible. However, if the Indigenous system is taken into account, sense of a kind emerges. These answers represent an attempt, from a local Indigenous viewpoint, to translate from the Indigenous system to the Anglo-Celtic.

In the Indigenous system, person 5v is person 1's M. The enumerators realised, however, that this person would not be classified as *mother* in the Anglo-Celtic system. On the SIHF, in attempting to solve the problem, the enumerators seem to have inverted the relationship: 'daughter' is probably a translation of ZC, which is what person 5v calls person 1. On the SIPF another solution was adopted: 'uncle' is the English term that locals most often use to translate MB (mother's brother). Person 6 is another M. Again, the enumerators realised that *mother* was not the appropriate Anglo-Celtic term. They aimed for an Anglo-Celtic term that picks out an M of a lower generation—but overshot by two generations.[16]

Fig. 3.7   Dwelling K: actual relationships of usual residents and visitor

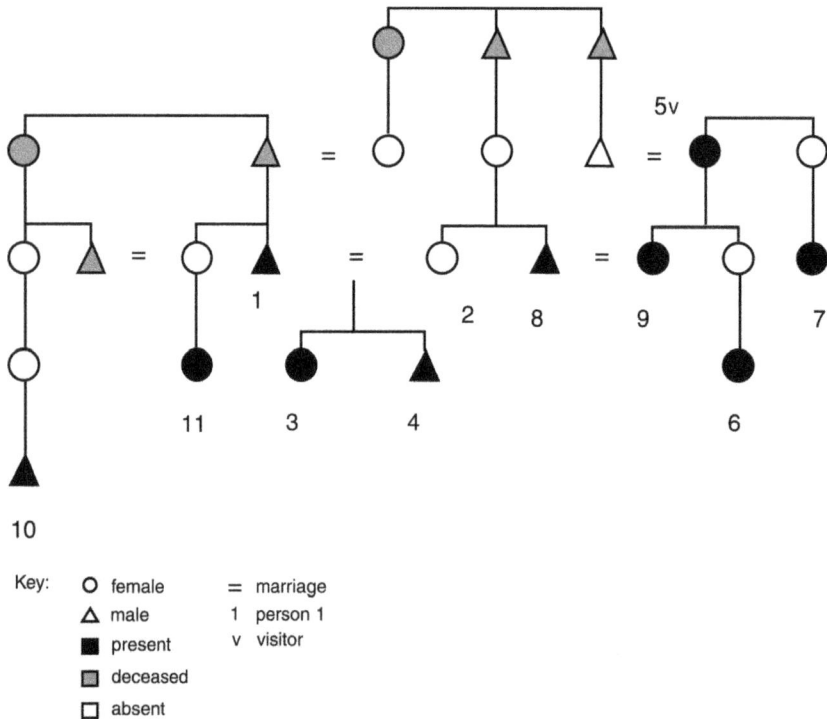

Key: O female   = marriage
       Δ male   1 person 1
       ■ present   v visitor
       ▣ deceased
       □ absent

'Sister's son-in-law' (as person 10 was described on his SIPF) was an attempt to translate the term (Z)DCFZC. The enumerators nearly got it right, but again they missed a generation. One possible rendering of (Z)DCFZC is 'sister's daughter's (potential or actual) son-in-law'.[17] Person 11 is person 1's sister's daughter. Person 11's as yet non-existent daughter would be person 10's MMBDD, and thus also his MBD, or potential wife.

In the case of person 9, the enumerators, perhaps suffering themselves from kinship fatigue at this point, attempted to opt for a 'straight' translation between the two systems. Person 8 is person 1's wife's brother, and so like her is person 1's MBC. This was 'correctly' translated as 'brother-in-law'. In the local system, the wife of a male MBC (i.e. person 9 in this case) is MM—a type of 'grand*mother*'.

Every single enumeration that I observed produced results of the kind described above. The census data, if coupled with the ethnographic data, offer a fascinating insight into the local Indigenous kinship system and principles of household formation, and into how local people think about and abstract principles from their kinship categories. But as raw data on household structure they are unusable, for two reasons. Firstly, the incommensurability of the two kinship systems results in 'relationship' data that reflects neither system, and which cannot be used to construct 'families' within households. Secondly, the implicit model upon which ABS household structures are predicated—the nuclear family—is a bad model for local Indigenous households in particular and, it could be argued, for Indigenous households in general.

The nuclear family deconstructed

The problem lies in the assumption that the nuclear family is a 'natural' structure that forms the basic social and coresidential unit in all cultures. Anglo-Celtic cultures tend to take the nuclear family as the 'norm', and to describe all other household types as variations on, or deviations from that norm. The ABS, as an institution of the Australian Anglo-Celtic mainstream, reflects that tendency in its definitions. The Anglo-Celtic kinship system, with its unique reciprocal terms for the members of the nuclear family, reinforces the view of the nuclear family as somehow 'natural'. In Fig. 3.8, each interior box surrounds an ego. The terms within the box are those by which other members of the Anglo-Celtic nuclear family address ego. The nuclear family and its constellation of relationships only comes into being with a marriage: any ego is likely to be a member of more than one nuclear family in their lifetime, first as a child (family of origin) and then as a parent (family of procreation).

Fig. 3.8 Anglo-Celtic kinship terminology and the nuclear family

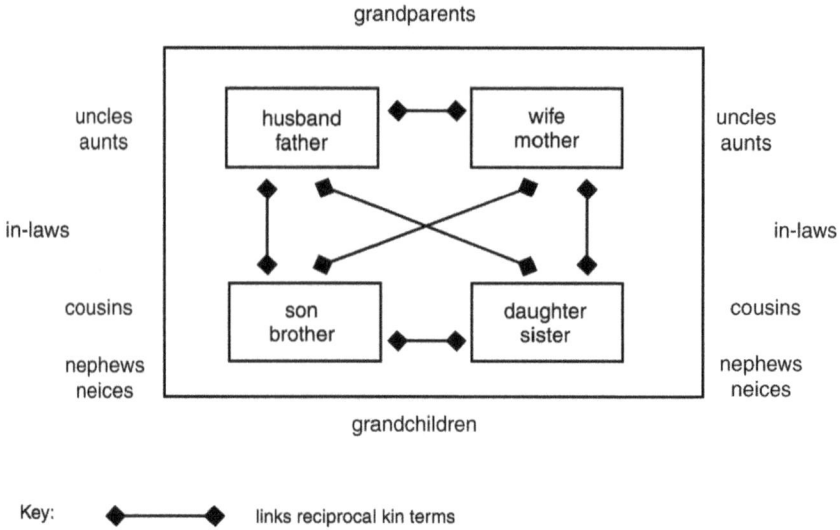

grandparents

| uncles
aunts | husband
father | wife
mother | uncles
aunts |

in-laws | | | in-laws

| cousins | son
brother | daughter
sister | cousins |

| nephews
neices | | | nephews
neices |

grandchildren

Key: ◆———◆ links reciprocal kin terms

The local Indigenous kinship system, in contrast, privileges lineages, not nuclear families (Fig. 3.9). Ego and ego's siblings are not primarily constituents of a nuclear family, but a point of intersection between an already existing patrilineage and matrilineage.

Fig. 3.9 Local Indigenous kinship terminology and the intersection of lineages

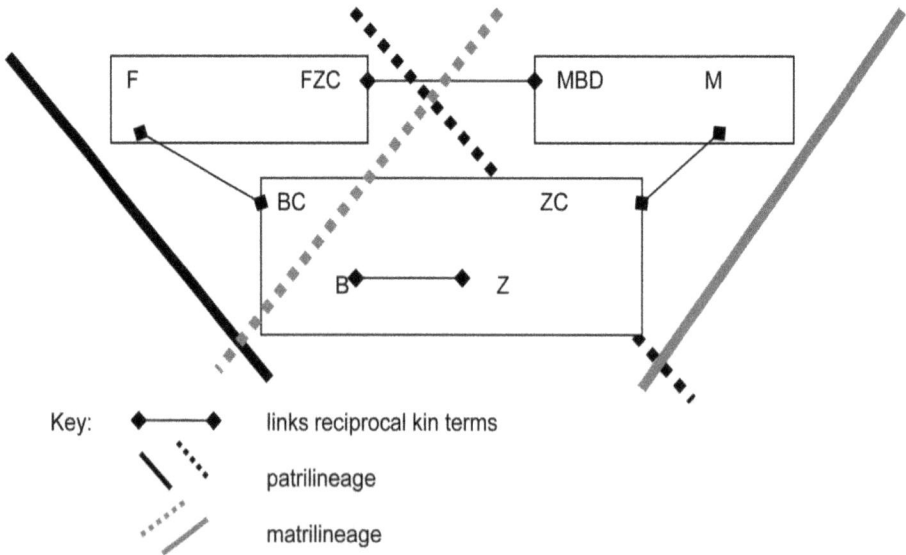

Key: ◆———◆ links reciprocal kin terms

▬ ▪▪▪ patrilineage

▬ ▪▪▪ matrilineage

The box in Fig. 3.9 does not represent an individual ego, but rather a contains a set of relationships that are constituted by the intersection of a patrilineage and a matrilineage in a particular generation. These relationships exist independent of any particular marriage because the FZC–MBC relationship between two people exists before a marriage does, and every person has many FZC and MBC. In Fig. 3.9 it is simply impossible to draw a box around a set of reciprocal terms that apply exclusively within a 'nuclear family'.[18] The siblings in the bottom box are BC with respect to their patrilineal parent, and ZC with respect to their matrilineal parent. The terms for sibling (B and Z) lie within the intersection of the two lineages that is constituted by the marriage.

A recommendation: back to basics

My first thoughts, as I sat observing, were that with more (and more theoretically informed) training it would be possible for local Indigenous people to produce results that would be interpretable in mainstream terms, at least for categories of kin that the mainstream system recognises as kin. Thinking in abstract terms about kinship is an everyday part of local life, and it would simply be a question of working out a systematic set of translation principles. But as I thought about it more, I began to question the premise upon which such a course of action would be based. What about kin who do not fit Anglo-Celtic categories? Would they be described as 'friends', or 'unrelated'—even if, in many cases they are addressed by the *same* kinship term as people considered to be kin in the Anglo-Celtic system? Would such a solution actually reflect the reality of the composition and dynamic of Indigenous households? It would not. It would simply represent an attempt to distort the Indigenous system by squeezing it into the mainstream Anglo-Celtic mould. And this particular local system is only one of many systems of kinship in Indigenous Australia. The same process would have to be implemented Australia-wide. This would be expensive, time-consuming, and logistically complex, if not impossible.

The better (and cheaper) course is to go back to first principles: for whom and for what purpose are these data on household composition being collected? The important generalisations that are being sought for comparative purposes concern the size of households in relation to the size of dwellings, their age and sex profiles, and whether or not people consider themselves to be related. It is not necessary to model this information in terms of nuclear family structure. Indigenous people tend to live in large multi-generational households, in which everyone is considered kin to everyone else: that is, in *extended family* households. This has been amply demonstrated in the literature (for recent and relevant data see Henry & Daly 2001; Musharbash 2001; Smith 2000a). The census cannot hope to uncover the difference and complexity of the local Indigenous kinship system, or any other Indigenous kinship system, in two questions, and it should not be attempting to do so. The number of persons in the household and the range of people's ages, would be enough to indicate whether or not Indigenous people are living in households that approach or diverge from mainstream norms.[19] If more fined-grained detail about particular sectors of the population is considered important, then those specific subgroups of the population could be targeted. For example, if ascertaining whether children are living in the same households as their 'real' parent(s) is considered important, then there could be questions targeted at those under 15 years old (and these could appear later in the form, after the question about age), asking whether their 'real' or 'actual' mother and/or father live in the dwelling.

Removing the emphasis on kinship would serve another valuable end. The case of the 'missing persons 1' highlights the central importance of kinship in local Indigenous life. To give it prime place on the census forms is to give people the impression that it is more important than anything else on the form, whereas, in fact, it is simply being used as a means to model certain kinds of demographic data.

Factors influencing the quality of the data

In the case of household structure and composition, the 2001 Census might be deemed guilty of trying too hard to accommodate the difference of Indigenous households. It failed in that it did not divorce itself sufficiently from the culture-specific categories of the Anglo-Celtic mainstream. The quality and interpretability of most of the data collected on the SIPFs are influenced systematically by the lack of knowledge and understanding in the wider society (as represented by the ABS) about the nature of Indigenous societies, and the ways in which they differ from 'mainstream' society. This is manifested in:

- the design of the forms and the manner in which the questions are presented;

- the content of some of the questions.

Equally significant is a corresponding lack of understanding on the part of local Indigenous people of the workings of mainstream society and of the intent behind the census, as it is reflected in the questionnaire. This is manifested in:

- a tendency to devote most effort to answering questions which are salient to them, and least effort to those which appear irrelevant;

- the misunderstanding of certain questions, resulting in answers very different from those that were intended to be elicited.

Some of these misunderstandings arose from the language used in posing the question (which could be seen as a weakness in the design of the questionnaire); others had their basis in cultural difference. Some were a combination of these, for context often provides clues to interpretation of language, and if the context is not understood then interpretation of language becomes harder. These issues could be addressed in the training of the enumerators, provided that the trainers were fully aware of what the potential problems might be.

The level of misunderstanding may have been exacerbated in the case of community A because the enumerators had not been fully familiarised with the SIPF before they started work. However, I do not think this was the most significant factor. As E1 said to me after the enumeration: 'we didn't really know the form at first, but we learned as we went along how to do them'. 'Training by doing' is the preferred local style: people are accustomed to learning in this way and are adept at it.

I turn now to a more detailed consideration of the data that were collected on 'age', 'place of residence', 'education', 'origin and ancestry', 'culture' (as measured by language use and religious affiliation), and 'work'. I will touch on several themes that bear on the quality of the data: the design of the form and of the questions, the content of the questions, and the relevance of some of the questions. For some of them prompt two questions in response. What is the purpose of this question? Who are these data being collected for?

How old are you?

Whereas most, if not all, non-Indigenous Australians know the precise date and year of their birth, even if they cannot remember their closest relatives' telephone numbers, exactly the reverse is true of most local Indigenous people. It is a question of what it is considered important to remember. The enumerators made valiant efforts to ascertain people's ages, and E1 was intending to check the answers later against the clinic records. I do not know if this actually happened, but if it did, it would still not have resulted in accurate date-of-birth information from some people, particularly the older ones. For example, one man gave his age (emphatically) as 63. His driver's licence records his birth date as 01/07/45, and the HA clinic records have his birth date as 01/01/48. Many older people have the first of January (or the first of July) as their birthday in the clinic records and on official documents. It can safely be inferred that such 'dates of birth' are guesstimates made by missionaries and other local record keepers.

There are local terms which designate degrees of maturity, or stages of life: [baby], [child], [circumcised boy], [prepubescent girl], [young man], and so on. Some terms from the mainstream have also been adopted locally, for example 'preschooler', 'schoolkid', and 'pensioner'. These terms all relate indirectly to age *ranges*. It might be better, therefore, to ask this question in a different way, giving people a choice of boxes to mark according to whether they were 0–5, 6–10, 11–15, and so on. It would be possible then, in training, to get the enumerators to match these up with the local terms for particular life stages. These could then be used to elicit the age data from the interviewees.[20]

'Place' of residence

Because the census is focused on the dwelling as the unit of analysis it cannot capture relationships between people who live in different dwellings. Does this matter? Every analyst who uses census data is aware that it is, above all, a dwelling-based survey and that it does not seek to provide data on inter-dwelling relationships.

However, many analysts may not be aware that Indigenous households can and sometimes do have members in more than one dwelling. In community A, as in many other Indigenous communities, the households of certain dwellings are linked closely to one another— economically as well as by ties of kinship. This is particularly true of dwellings containing a man and dwellings of the wives with whom he is not presently cohabiting. The people at community A rejected 'separated but not divorced' as the correct box to mark for this scenario. The SIPF is neutral on the question of polygamy (either by design or by accident). It is not possible to answer the question on marriage (Q. 6) in a way that indicates how many wives a man has, or how many co-wives a woman has. As we have seen, at community A there are, apparently, two dwellings where person 1 is a married woman with children, but where there is no 'husband' on the scene. These data might be interpreted to indicate the presence of 'single parent' households, with all that this implies in mainstream society. This would be a misinterpretation, since these are not deserted and disadvantaged women struggling to raise their children in isolation. They and their children are part of an extended family that happens to occupy more than one dwelling—and indeed it is not uncommon to find some of the children of one co-wife living in the dwelling of another.

The dwelling is not the salient 'unit of residence' at community A; rather the community itself is. This much was clear in the enumerators' and respondents' reactions to Q. 7–9, with the recurring demand for postal addresses. Even larger communities such as B are almost invariably divided into recognised sub-communities or 'camps' (e.g. Top Camp, Bottom Camp). The design of the SIPF should perhaps acknowledge this fact, by using 'community' or 'sub-community' instead of 'place' and by eliminating requests for postal addresses. The subdivisions of big communities could be identified as part of the training of the enumerators.

The data collected at community A on where people were living one and five years ago are almost certainly unreliable. One problem is the concept of 'X number of years ago', since local people do not measure their lives in such terms. Solutions to this problem might be found in the training of the enumerators, as in the case of the 'age' and 'place' questions. It might simply be a matter of impressing upon them that the ABS considers this information to be important, and devising more appropriate, locally salient cues, such as particular memorable events that were of importance to community members.[21]

There is another, more intractable problem: for local people, these questions about 'place' are not value-free, as they are for most non-Indigenous Australians. Place is not just physical space. People have strong spiritual and emotional attachments to particular places, and if they are now living at one of those places they are more than likely to state that this is where they have always lived 'most of the time', thus understating their mobility.

Ancestral connections

The questions on origins and ancestry need rethinking. In their present form they are underpinned by covert distinctions—'Indigenous' as opposed to 'ethnic' as opposed to 'unmarked' (Anglo-Celtic mainstream). Of these, the 'Indigenous' is the most marked, because it is referred to in two separate questions, and the Anglo-Celtic mainstream is so 'unmarked' that it is not even mentioned. From the Indigenous perspective this makes no sense, and although the responses were accurate—or appeared to be—the questions were felt to be decidedly odd. For Indigenous people, 'Indigenous' is the unmarked category, and the Anglo-Celtic mainstream is the most marked, because it is the most common source of non-Indigenous ancestry for local Indigenous people.

What precisely is the information being sought by the question on origin? It is not clear to me, and it certainly was not clear to the local Indigenous people. Is it another question about ancestry in a different guise, or a question about self-identification?

What is a language?

It is important for the designers of the IES to be aware of issues that are potentially loaded in a political sense. The bilingual education program in the Northern Territory was recently under real threat. One argument that can be used to challenge the viability of such programs is that it is just too difficult to cater for communities where many different languages are spoken. This is not an argument that can seriously be mounted at communities where the language in question is spoken, but the data from the 2001 Census, in the hands of non-specialists, could be used to support this argument. It would have been a simple matter to instruct the enumerators to enter the term that has been coined for the language (by linguists) as the language spoken by all speakers of a dialect of that language. In terms of providing salient information for policy-makers this would have been the best option (although for the sociolinguist the data that were actually collected are much more fascinating).

The 2001 data issued by the ABS in its first release indicates that nearly 20 per cent of Indigenous respondents at HA outstations said they spoke 'English only'. This does not correspond in any way to reality: I can think of no local Indigenous individual in this region who does not speak an Aboriginal language as their first language.

'Religion' and 'beliefs'

If the question on religion had carried the explicit instruction that more than one box could be marked, the answers would have been a more accurate reflection of the situation at community A. The term 'Traditional Beliefs' carries an implicit value judgment: beliefs do not have the same status as religion unless they are regarded (and described) as a 'belief system'.

The data in the first ABS release of the 2001 Census indicate that fewer than 40 per cent of the Indigenous population of the HA outstations marked 'Traditional Beliefs' as their religion. This does not accord with my own observations of the Indigenous people of this region, who continue strongly to maintain their traditional belief system and their ceremonial life. The design of the question on the SIPF almost certainly materially influenced the response.

Education: what's in a name?

Most of the questions on schooling and further training and education were difficult for community A enumerators and residents to understand and answer, and this generalisation probably holds for many Indigenous communities in 'remote' Australia. Yet arguably, accurate and interpretable data are vital for policy formulation in this area, which will have a strong influence on the future wellbeing and self-sufficiency of discrete Indigenous communities. No matter how the questions are formulated, the training of the enumerators needs to focus on their content. The enumerators need to be given the knowledge to interpret the responses of the interviewees, most of whom have not received formal education past the primary level of schooling. Those who have further training of some sort mostly fall into the category 'Yes, other course' in Q. 23. In such cases it should be possible to sidestep the next four questions.

'Work' and CDEP

Most adults at community A are on CDEP. The status of the CDEP as a provider of 'real work' is politically contested (see e.g. Shergold 2001). The SIPF for the 2001 Census unequivocally equates CDEP with other kinds of work, starting at Q. 29 with the question: 'Did you have a paid job last week?' and providing a box for 'Yes, worked—CDEP'. In the questions which follow, almost to the end of the form (Q. 30–38), the interviewee is led, inexorably, further down this path. The SIPF makes valiant attempts to keep all these questions relevant to CDEP 'jobs' but the effort shows, for example in Q. 34: 'What work does your employer do? (If worked for CDEP write 'community council')'.

The way in which these questions are put creates a double bind for local people, because CDEP is not primarily payment for work in the outstation context—at least not for the kind of work contained in the prompts to Q. 30. CDEP payments are nevertheless vital to people who live on outstations, since they are the main source of regular cash income. It is therefore quite unsurprising that the answers to the questions on 'work' were formulaic.

Although the 'rubbish collectors' certainly keep this particular community clean and tidy, the job does not represent 20 hours of work per week for several young men. The inference that may be drawn by some is that CDEP is 'sit-down' money. The inhabitants of community A do not spend an undue amount of time sitting around doing nothing, but the prompts for Q. 30 create no space for people to mention the work that they spend most time doing. A point made by Diane Smith is pertinent here:

> Serious problems arise for government policy and programs, and for their clients, when supposedly objective statistical data do not adequately represent, or only partially represent, social and economic realities. Associated with such difficulties is the tendency to dismiss as unimportant those processes and behaviours which we do not know how to measure by standard measures (1992: 68).

Hunting and gathering are daily activities for most young 'rubbish collectors' at community A. And if these are implicitly discounted as work, how much more so is working for the community during ceremonial performance? The same young 'rubbish collectors' spend sometimes up to six hours a day dancing energetically and skilfully in the hot sun, for days at a time. Such skills, and prowess at hunting and fishing, are the product of long hours of learning and practice, and the work that results contributes significantly to the physical and cultural wellbeing of the community. The focus in the SIPF on the mainstream notion of 'work' devalues these 'traditional' forms of work. The failure to provide a space for their inclusion does two things: it implies that this kind of work does not contribute to the economic and social wellbeing of the individuals and their community, and it allows those who are so minded to characterise Aboriginal people as getting 'something for nothing'.

There are two possible solutions. If CDEP is categorised as work, then traditional forms of work, such as hunting, fishing, collecting bush tucker and making art should be included in the prompt to the question: 'What job did you do?' And it should be possible to list more that one job.

Alternatively, CDEP in places like community A should perhaps be uncoupled from the notion of work in the mainstream sense, and from the labour force statistics. A desirable side effect would be that the SIPF, for people on CDEP, would be much shorter. If this solution were adopted there should be an additional question on the SIPF that allows people to estimate the extent and nature of their 'unpaid' work. Art and craft production, which is one of the only other significant sources of cash income, should be included in the prompts for non-CDEP work: its presence might cause (a few) people to reflect a bit more closely on the sources of their cash income, and to make some effort to record them.

Conclusion

The effectiveness of the IES can be measured according to several criteria. The strategy for the recruitment of the Indigenous enumerators appears to have been effective, particularly when one bears in mind the disruptions that occurred. The strategies for eliminating under-enumeration and double counting were about as good as they could be, in circumstances that are inherently extremely difficult. Some fine-tuning in these areas is probably possible and desirable, but radical rethinking is not required.

Because I was not able to observe a training session, and because the training of the enumerators at community A was curtailed, it is difficult to comment directly on training procedures and content, and their effects. In the recommendations below I suggest quite radical changes to the form and content of the SIPF. If implemented, the training of the CFOs and enumerators would need to change in any case, and therefore:

- I would strongly recommend that any new version of the SIHF and/or SIPF be pre-tested in the field in a range of communities, using as enumerators people who were employed as enumerators in the 2001 Census. They, in conjunction with a CFO who had also taken part in the 2001 Census exercise and an anthropologically-trained observer would be in the best position, between them, to evaluate the form and make recommendations for any further refinements. Such an exercise could also act as a pilot for new training procedures. Such training should focus as much on the contents of the questions on the SIHF/SIPF as on procedural matters.

Detailed recommendations concerning the form and content of the questions have been made throughout the second half of this paper. The following, more general, recommendations flow from them:

- The SIPF is much too long. Administering it was an onerous task for the enumerators, and this encouraged formulaic responses to certain questions, particularly ones whose purpose was opaque to local people, or which were worded or structured in ways that made them hard to interpret.

- The presence of questions on kinship at the beginning of the SIPF, and the fact that they also appeared on the SIHF, gave them undue emphasis. Because kinship is such a salient topic for local people, they took this as a signal that these were the most important questions to address, and more time was spent on Q.4, and on thinking about how it should be answered, than on any other question. I have suggested that the idiom of kinship be dispensed with in eliciting information on household composition, and that a new type of extended family household be added to the inventory of ABS household types.

- The SIHF and the SIPFs for the dwelling should possibly be combined, as they are in the 'mainstream' form. However, the summary information gathered on 'absent usual residents' and 'visitors' is valuable, and should be retained. The SIHF might be retained as a separate document, but in another guise, as a 'household checklist'. This is how it was used by the enumerators at community A, and it proved a useful tool.

- The layout of the SIPF needs attention. The use of large, bold print versus small print should be carefully reviewed, bearing in mind that many Indigenous people (including many enumerators) are not fluent readers of English. The repetitive demands to supply postal addresses (for dwellings and places of work) should be circumvented.

- The design of the pathways through the form also needs some further thought. One possibility is to uncouple CDEP from the labour force data so that CDEP participants do not have to answer numerous questions about their 'work'. The questions on further education and training could also be streamlined.

- More thought should be given to devising questions that allow 'non-mainstream' aspects of Indigenous social life to emerge from the data. In some cases this simply involves putting more thought into the prompts to a question, to allow a wider range of options in the response. The overall impression given by the data on the SIPF is that the people of community A 'lack' certain things in comparison with the mainstream—education and 'real jobs' in particular. If the concept of Australia as a multicultural society is to be taken seriously, then an instrument such as the census should be attempting to capture, as far as possible, significant features of non-mainstream cultures that the *mainstream* culture lacks, particularly those that influence interaction with the mainstream in significant domains such as welfare, employment and education.

- Further to this, a certain amount of 'deconstruction' of mainstream categories would not go amiss. The 'nuclear family' is a case in point. Another is the way in which different sectors of the population are categorised in the questions on 'origin' and 'ancestry'.

Many of these suggestions, if taken up, would result in a shorter and more 'culture-specific' form, tailored to those Indigenous people who live in discrete communities on or near their traditional 'country', with limited or no access to the labour market. These are communities where the major organising principle of social life is kinship, where households tend to be large, compositionally complex, multi-generational and somewhat fluid in composition because of high levels of individual mobility, and where non-mainstream forms of 'work' make an important contribution to the local economy and to cultural life. This might, perforce, narrow the scope for the administration of the IES by enumerators. Other

Indigenous people might be candidates for a self-administered IES form, or would be required to fill in the mainstream form, with help from an enumerator if needed.

Such a strategy would not be without its own problems: Indigenous Australia was never homogeneous, and the contemporary situation there is even more diversity as a result of the vagaries of the colonial process and the uneven penetration of the settler culture and its institutions. The terms 'remote', 'rural' and 'urban', with which the settler society attempts model this diversity, once reflected a certain logic of distance. Today, however, these terms are becoming increasingly metaphorical. A 'remote' community may find itself cheek by jowl with the company town—and the mine—of a multinational enterprise. 'Rural' Kuranda and 'remote' Yuendumu are different in many respects, but have a 'number of fundamental commonalities', including the fact that: 'the concept of "family" based on the extended family formation is the central and abiding social and economic construct, and a key component of individual identity' (Smith 2000b: 95). The ABS would have to assess each region, each community within a region, and even individuals within communities to determine which was the most appropriate means of enumeration for them. But the result would be a far higher proportion of self-administered forms, and the collection of much more reliable and relevant data on a sector of the Australian population that will continue to be not only highly distinctive but also in great need of well informed state policy and programs.

Notes

1. CHINS provides an estimate of the service population rather than a census-style head count. CHINS estimates invariably, therefore, produce larger populations than does the census enumeration.

2. It may have been a deliberate strategy to give E4 this house, but unfortunately it did not occur to me to check this. At the time the dwellings were apportioned I was not aware of the potential problem.

3. This process sometimes presented a challenge to my position as a neutral 'observer': it was hard for the enumerators not to cast me as a 'helper'. From the time of the 'training' session onwards I was appealed to intermittently for clarification on particular questions. I resisted giving advice as best I could (by pleading ignorance, and saying they should ask the CFO or the CC), except in the area of the translation of kinship terms. Here I simply followed where they led: they were bent on devising English 'translations' for local kinship terms that have no English equivalents, rather than classifying as non-kin people whom they regard as kin.

4. Daly and Smith's discussion of the interview techniques devised for community case studies at Kuranda and Yuendumu is pertinent here: 'The social pool of people contributing as additional de facto "respondents" to each questionnaire were included in the interview process…This approach…is positively oriented to socially embedded and constructed Indigenous modes of communication where the individual cannot be effectively "quarantined" for the purposes of eliciting information' (2000: 20). The enumerators at community A were, in effect, applying the same technique.

5. The form of Q. 2, which is not a direct question (Sex:) betrays the presence of a topic that the compiler of the questionnaire (presumably a member of the Euro-Australian mainstream), found inappropriate as the subject of a direct question. None of us is free of cultural taboos.

6. From day two onwards, E1 took a calculator with him. When someone knew their year of birth, this was subtracted from 2001, and the answer was recorded as the person's age.

7. Most local marriages would be classified as de facto relationships in mainstream terms, but it would be quite inappropriate, in the view of local Indigenous people, to classify them thus. The category 'de facto' occurs neither on the SIPF nor on the mainstream SIHF, and perhaps the injunction '"Married" refers to registered marriages', which does *not* appear on the SIPF, should also be removed from the *mainstream* HF.

8. The word Dreaming is not used in this area, but the word translated here as 'sacred ancestral inheritance' corresponds more or less to what mainstream Australia understands by that concept.

9. In contrast to the situation in some other parts of Australia (see David Martin, this volume), local people in this area attach no cultural value to fluency in English. Being able to speak English is seen as a useful skill, but inability to do so is not valued negatively.

10. The actual amount of money that people get in their account each fortnight varies, because the HA deducts money from people's CDEP payments to cover their outstanding bills before crediting the remainder to their account.

11. The fourth box in Q. 29 refers to 'sorry business' as a possible reason for being off work. People in this area do not use this phrase to describe funerals, and I suspect that there are other places in Australia where it is also an unfamiliar usage. It would be better to use a standard English term such as 'funeral'.

12. I was told this by one of the absent 'usual residents'.

13. The *2001 Census Dictionary* (ABS 2001) defines a person's usual residence as the place where the person 'has lived or intends to live for a total of six months or more'.

14. When I returned to community A in June 2002, at least one tent which had been erected just after the census enumeration in 2001 was still in place outside its associated dwelling. It had acquired a protective awning consisting of a large tarpaulin on a bush timber frame.

15. This is not to say that people do not distinguish between their actual mother (and other 'close' M such as their mother's sisters) and other M, in terms of sentiment and behaviour.

16. In the great-grandchild's generation, female children are merged under the terms M or FZ, depending on the patrilineage to which they belong.

17. As mentioned previously, E1 and I had several conversations about how to translate (Z)DCFZC. On one occasion he reasoned that the reciprocal term MBCMM means 'mother-in-law's mother', so in English its reciprocal term should be 'mother-in-laws' son's son-in-law'. This actually works for a MBCMM and a male DCFZC, but whereas E1 made the computation instantly in his head, I had to go away and puzzle over a kinship chart for some time to confirm it for myself. This is not necessarily because E1 is smarter than I am (although that may well be true). Rather, a 'first' kinship system is like a first language: the individual 'born into' the system carries its grammar unconsciously in their head. A 'second' kinship system is like a second language: the rules must be learned consciously and laboriously, and full fluency is extremely hard to achieve.

18. Many other features of the kinship terminology support the thesis that a major organising principle of the system is the relationship between lineages over time. These will be discussed in another paper.

19. Diane Smith (pers. comm.) suggests an alternative strategy: getting the enumerators to draw up genealogies for each dwelling. In this way, household structures would be recoverable in finer detail. However, such a strategy would require extra training for the enumerators, would add to the time that it takes to complete the SIHF, and would be easily implemented only in communities where the enumerators were well known to the interviewees, and where the enumerators themselves were familiar with the details of how everyone was related to each other. Moreover, a small proportion of local people are in 'wrong' marriages, or are the children of such unions, and such information has to be treated carefully. While everyone in a community is aware of such facts, it is not usual or acceptable to discuss them openly in public.

20. Roger Jones (pers. comm.) doubts whether this would produce data that was any more accurate. However, an 'age-range' as opposed to an 'exact age' question would be more in tune with how local people view the question of age, and the results would certainly be *no less* accurate.

21. The local language distinguishes six seasons in the year; 'dry season' is not one of them. For most locals the year of the last census would not be memorable for that particular reason.

4. Adapting to circumstance: the 2001 Census in the Alice Springs town camps

Will Sanders

Introduction

The Australian national census of population and housing is conducted every five years by the ABS. It attempts to collect basic demographic and socioeconomic information about the total Australian population and various subsets of that population, such as Indigenous Australians. As Indigenous Australians are a small minority of all Australians whose circumstances can differ considerably from those of the majority population, the ABS has over recent censuses adopted a special enumeration strategy for Indigenous Australians, particularly in the discrete Indigenous communities in sparsely settled northern and central Australia. The elements of this IES have been in place in the Northern Territory since 1976, Western Australia and South Australia since 1981 and in Queensland since 1991 (see Taylor 1993, and this volume; Loveday & Wade-Marshall 1985). They involve special Indigenous household and personal questionnaires which are designed for interview-based completion, rather than the self-completion of a single household questionnaire relied on in the larger population. Interviewers, or census collectors, are often recruited through Indigenous organisations and are usually themselves Indigenous. CCs, who oversee interviewers, are also recruited through contact with Indigenous community organisations and may also be Indigenous. CCs also undertake work on a third special Indigenous form, the Dwelling Check List, for each discrete Indigenous community.

Through the IES an attempt has clearly been made by the ABS to work in consultation and cooperation with local Indigenous organisations and individuals, as well as to develop a questionnaire procedure which is more appropriate to the circumstances of those being counted. Despite these efforts, doubts about the adequacy of census information relating to Indigenous Australians have continued to be raised. Indigenous community organisations have frequently suggested, when presented with census figures, that their community has been under-enumerated. Researchers too have had cause to suggest under enumeration and other data inadequacies (see for example Taylor 1993, Martin & Taylor 1995). As a result, it seemed useful to attempt to observe the conduct of the 2001 Census in some of these discrete Indigenous communities where the special enumeration strategy was to be used. This paper reports on the conduct of the 2001 Census in the Aboriginal town camps of Alice Springs.

Background

The town camps of Alice Springs provide a living space for Aboriginal people which is considerably different from general suburban housing. At their least developed, the camps can be a series of officially-unrecognised improvised humpies. Nowadays, however, most camps are considerably more developed and recognised than this, with some security of land tenure, some community facilities such as running water, lighting and ablution blocks and some more formally constructed dwellings, be they perhaps only basic tin sheds. At their most developed, the Alice Springs town camps have some of the characteristics of low-cost residential housing estates, with toilets and other facilities in individual houses, a clear block and road layout and house numbers, if not street names.

The town camps in Alice Springs have been assisted in their development over the last 25 years by the Tangentyere Council, an Aboriginal organisation specifically established for this purpose. Tangentyere now services and assists 19 town camps which are spread across Alice Springs, predominantly on its outskirts but also in some instances in small areas nearer the centre of town (see Fig 4.1).

The ABS approached Tangentyere during the first half of 2001 seeking its cooperation and assistance in the conduct of the census in the Alice Springs town camps. The initial reaction from Tangentyere was not very positive. Past censuses had not been particularly useful to Tangentyere. They had not identified the town camps as distinct collection districts (CDs) and so little or no information could be extracted from past censuses relating specifically to the town camps. Tangentyere's reaction became more positive when it was explained to them by the ABS's central Australian census manager that CDs in Alice Springs for the 2001 census had been re-designed so as to separate out the town camps. Eleven identifiable CDs covered the 19 town camps serviced by Tangentyere, some covering only one town camp and some covering two or three town camps close together in a particular area of town (see Fig. 4.1).

Tangentyere agreed to do what it could to assist the ABS with the conduct of the census. It undertook to provide the ABS with the list of dwellings in the town camps for which it attempted to charge rent in order to help with the construction of Dwelling Check Lists for the 19 town camps. It also undertook to provide a training room and to provide ABS with access to a pool of potential local Aboriginal workers through its Job Shop and general networks. It was also agreed that two Tangentyere staff members from the housing section would be dedicated full time for two weeks to the census collection process on a cost recovery basis. All this was arranged while the central Australian census manager, a permanent ABS employee, was still based in Darwin, 1,600 kilometres to the north, there being no permanent ABS office in central Australia.

Getting going

The ABS's central Australian census manager arrived in Alice Springs in mid June 2001 and began gearing up the operation. The plan for the discrete Aboriginal communities, both in Alice Springs and out bush, was to conduct the census over a period of perhaps two or three weeks in the month before the official census day on 7 August. The intention was to avoid the complication of a major movement of people from these communities to the Yuendumu Sports Weekend on 4–6 August. A related aim was to enumerate people over a period of time in a fairly usual place of residence, rather than just somewhere they happened to be visiting on a particular night.

Fig. 4.1   Alice Springs Community Living Areas, with hand annotations of town camp CD numbers

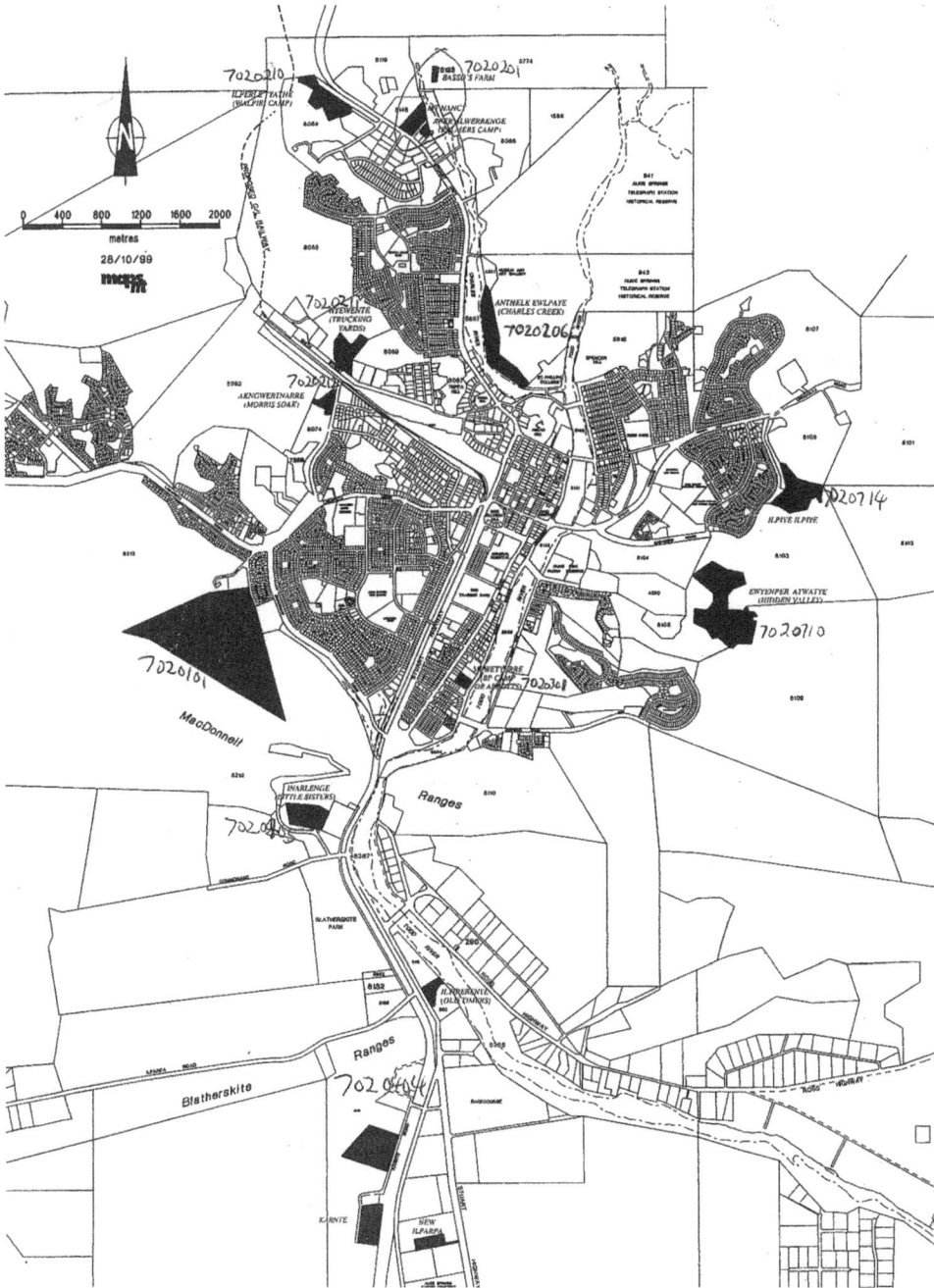

Source: NT Department of Lands / Maps NT

The time-frame of this plan began gradually to change when it proved somewhat more difficult to recruit interviewer-collectors (henceforth interviewers) and CCs for the town camps than had first been anticipated. Four potential CCs had been identified by the ABS's central Australian census manager in conjunction with Tangentyere, two of whom were the Tangentyere housing employees, one of whom was an ex-Tangentyere employee now working with another Aboriginal organisation in town, and one of whom was a former long-term Department of Social Security officer. All were, at least partly, of Aboriginal descent and were well known in the area. At an initial strategy meeting and training session for CCs organised for 7 July, only one of the four turned up, along with the Tangentyere housing manager. At a second training session organised for 20 July, only the two who were not employees of Tangentyere showed up and it was soon ascertained that the two Tangentyere employees had decided they could not combine census collection with their current employment responsibilities relating to housing work.

This training session went well, with both coordinators clearly catching on quickly to the nature of the task they were being asked to undertake. One indicated that he was somewhat restricted in the time he could devote to the job, because of his employment elsewhere. But the other was not otherwise employed and had more time at his disposal. Both were asked to try and find other Aboriginal people who might be interested in being interviewers and a number of possible times for an interviewer training session were identified a week to ten days hence. It was also decided that the central Australian census manager should try to meet the Tangentyere Executive Council the following week to try to build some more support within Tangentyere for the census collection process now that it was imminent.

As well as hoping that the two CCs would be able to come up with Aboriginal people who might be interested in being interviewers, the central Australian census manager also put in some time over the next week encouraging the Tangentyere Job Shop to refer people on to him. An interviewer training session was finally organised for 31 July and five potential interviewers and the two CCs attended. This training session went for three to four hours. All the participants seemed interested and to be picking up the idea of the work quite quickly, but the training was as yet incomplete as none had themselves practiced filling in actual census forms. The training session was called to a halt around 1.30 p.m. as the seven participants all felt they had had enough for one day, and a continuation of the session was organised for the next morning. Only three of the five newly-recruited potential interviewers showed up the next day to complete the training, together with one of the two CCs. All went well, although there were some interesting issues raised during the process of practising filling out forms. These are worthy of further discussion so they can be revisited in the light of actual collection experience.

Starting with the SIHF, the central Australian census manager emphasised that the ABS in the Northern Territory was trying to enumerate primarily on a usual residence basis in these discrete Aboriginal communities. This meant, he explained, that all people who had lived in a dwelling in a community for more than six months of the previous year or were likely to live there for more than six months of the next year could be counted as 'people who live here', the language the SIHF used to describe usual residents (see

Appendix B). He also noted that visitors or 'people who are staying here' should also be listed on the SIHF, but that if they were also likely to be counted elsewhere they did not need a SIPF filled out for them. Some visitors would require a SIPF, but some would not. The count, on the SIPFs, was thus to be usual residents plus *some* visitors, though *all* visitors present were to be listed on the SIHFs. This seemed reasonably clear and well understood.

A little further on in discussion of the SIHF, it was suggested by one or two of the trainees that it might be difficult to get a figure for the rent paid for the house from any one individual interviewee, as the Tangentyere rent policy was partly a per person contribution scheme and not just a single, clear per house rent. It was suggested that perhaps the rental information should be obtained direct from Tangentyere, rather than from the interviewees and that this could tie in with the construction of the Dwelling Check Lists. As noted above, the Dwelling Check Lists which were being drawn up for the town camps were derived from Tangentyere's administrative records and covered any dwelling for which Tangentyere was attempting to collect some rent.

There was also some discussion of the issue of age and the fact that some Aboriginal people might not know their age precisely. It was however agreed that they might know their year of birth, from which age could be calculated, but that if they did not, an estimate of age could be made from discussing with them other people and events.

Another question which caused some concern was the income question (Q. 28, see Appendix C) on the SIPF. It was felt that the distinction between before and after tax would not be made and some people may say what they get weekly, as Tangentyere CDEP employees are paid weekly, and that a quick calculation would need to be made. Some of the concern about this question was allayed when the collectors realised that they did not have to obtain precise income figures, but merely had to place people in pre-determined categories. Some discussion ensued as to which of these income categories people on various Centrelink payments and CDEP would probably be in.

Another question which caused comment, rather than concern, was whether the person had looked for a job in the last four weeks. It was generally agreed that not many of the people in the town camps would be actively looking for work, as there was not much work around that they had any chance of obtaining, but that they would probably say they were looking for work if they were on Newstart Payments because that was what the conditions of payment required them to say when asked that question by Centrelink.

At the end of this second morning of training it was agreed that the three collectors and one CC were ready to start. It was agreed for all to meet the next morning at nine o'clock at a particular small town camp and to 'have a go' before the people there started moving around for the day. It was generally agreed that early morning was going to be the best time of day to get people in the camps because of movement out of the camps to other places in town later in the day and also because of drinking going on in the camps later in the day.

The next day, Thursday 2 August, only two of the three fully-trained interviewers turned up at the small town camp for the first collection, and the third never returned. There was at that point no Dwelling Check List for this camp, as there were no dwellings there for which Tangentyere was attempting to collect rent. The CC set about constructing a Dwelling Check List by looking around. There were five tin sheds without internal services and two sets of communal ablution blocks and toilets. Meanwhile one of the interviewers had approached one of the tin sheds and was beginning to complete a SIHF for it. A 'Person 1' was identified, somewhat arbitrarily, and others who had obviously spent the previous night sleeping in or around that tin shed were gradually added. Others, who had not so obviously slept in or around this tin shed the previous night but perhaps somewhere else around the camp, also came over and offered their names. Soon the SIHF contained a list of 14 people, and the interviewer and CC realised that it was perhaps becoming more of a communal personal checklist. The CC and the interviewer decided to abandon the idea of separate households in this small camp and just to work on this one SIHF. At that point, after about 15 minutes' work, the addition of people to this single SIHF was halted and attention was switched to filling out SIPFs for the 14 people now listed on the form.

Both interviewers now worked on the filling in of SIPFs for these 14 people for about two hours, while the CC, who did not himself fill out SIPFs, provided support by calling people back to have their forms done and fielding questions about how answers to questions should be treated; for example what sorts of training courses qualified for a 'yes' answer in the post-school education questions, since many of these people had over the years undertaken some training course or another. By 11.15 a.m. SIPFs had been completed for 12 of the 14 people on the single SIHF, while the other two, it was indicated, had 'walked away' from the camp to do something else. One of the collectors, who lived at an adjacent town camp, agreed to come back at another time to try and track down these two. The people at the camp had begun to lose interest in the census collection process and no more were offering themselves to be put on either the existing single SIHF or on a new one. The interviewers too were tired and they did not actively try to identify and pursue any other individuals who might still be in the camp but not on the first SIHF. The CC and the interviewers agreed to adjourn for the day and the two interviewers agreed that they would continue on their own in other camps with which they were familiar the next day.

During that first morning's work I had, as an observer, noted 25 people in that camp at about 9.15 a.m. When I mentioned this to the central Australian census manager, he in turn mentioned it to the CC who replied that it had been ascertained that the other people in the camp that morning were just visitors and therefore did not need to be counted. If the principles enunciated in training had been followed, these visitors would of course have been listed on SIHFs and then divided into those who did and those who did not require a SIPF depending on whether they were likely to be counted elsewhere. But in practice, with the overall collection task proving somewhat time consuming and arduous, the idea of someone being a visitor was used by interviewers and the CC as a rationale for not listing them even on a SIHF, thereby reducing the task at hand to slightly more manageable proportions. The emphasis was, after all, as they had been told in training, on counting people where they are usual residents.

We will return to these issues later. But as an observer of the collection at that first camp that first day, I should perhaps say that I was not entirely convinced by the line of argument that the other 11 people in the camp that morning were visitors. I had observed some discussion about particular people who were present that morning not 'belonging' there. However, from the way this was said I had interpreted it to mean as much that they were not particularly welcome at the camp, as that they did not usually live there or were not currently staying there. Indeed, it seemed likely that the forceful assertion of their not 'belonging' probably reflected the fact that they had stayed there a while, uninvited, and were likely to continue doing so for some time to come. The likelihood of their being counted elsewhere in the census was at least questionable. And the census had now been done in this camp, except for the issue of returning to get SIPFs for the last two people on the single SIHF.

Twelve days in August: building the effort

On Friday 3 August, I accompanied one of the two fully-trained and now practically-experienced interviewers to another town camp to begin the count there. This was a more developed camp with a block and street layout and houses numbered from one up into the twenties, but no street names. We approached one of the houses which had people visibly in and around it that morning and the collector asked for the person whose name was listed against this house on the Dwelling Check List derived from the Tangentyere housing list. It was quickly ascertained that this person no longer lived there and that others had taken over. A middle-aged man offered himself as household spokesperson and, through that process, became nominated as 'Person 1' for the SIHF. Once more, there followed a 15-minute process of adding household members' names, genders, ages and relationships to a SIHF. What emerged was an extended family household of middle-aged brothers and sisters and their partners, and a more elderly father of those brothers and sisters. There were no children physically evident at the household and an inquiry about this elicited the response that the children were back in communities out bush. This was largely an adults' place for town-based living, including a fair bit of drinking, although clearly the links with communities and children out bush were quite strong and frequent. Indeed while we were there a taxi load of five more people arrived at the house, complete with blankets and including two children. Also one of the adults present offered the information that he and some others were that afternoon heading out to Yuendumu for the sports weekend and that they might not be back for a while.

Once the initial process of filling out the SIHF had been completed, attention turned once again to filling out SIPFs. Four were completed within an hour and before people started wandering off and doing other things for the day. By 10.15 a.m. the collector was having trouble getting those listed on the SIHF to sit with him and do a SIPF. They had contributed to the filling in of the SIHF, watched two or three people do SIPFs and were now losing interest in the process. The interviewer too was getting tired and did not want to have to push people. We adjourned from the camp for a break and for the interviewer to buy some more cigarettes. He had just given away half a packet as a part of the process of interesting people in the census collection process!

When I adjourned to my office I wrote the following in my field journal:

> It strikes me that the most problematic part of this collection process is keeping up the interest of the respondents and, to a lesser extent, the collectors. This interviewer, who is good, got half a household done this morning before he and they needed a break. At that rate, with only two interviewers up and running at this stage, this census could take months. The likely result is a very significant undercount as people just avoided putting themselves forward to the collectors, or simply never come in contact with them.

I wondered whether SIPFs would ever be obtained for the six other people in that morning's dwelling who had been listed on the SIHF, since some were now heading off to Yuendumu, and whether the family that had arrived in the taxi with their blankets would ever be counted. They were now staying at a house where, like the small camp of the day before, the census had for all intents and purposes largely been done, though there were still SIPFs for that household which needed to be filled out.

The central Australian census manager was, at this stage of proceedings, very much aware that he needed to get more interviewers working in the town camps. He had initially been aiming for between eight and ten interviewers, on the assumption that they could each complete between 100 and 200 forms over a two or three week period and thus potentially together count somewhere between 1,000 and 1,500 people in the Alice Springs town camps. Tangentyere had over recent years attempted some very basic counts of its own which had indicated a town camp population of between 800 and 1,300 and this had formed the basis for the census manager's approach. However the initial recruitment and training drive had not yielded anything like this number of interviewers. Another attempt would have to be made.

At this point, the attention of the central Australian census manager was fairly fully taken up with the upcoming conduct of the larger, more general census only four days away. He did, however, manage to recruit three more potential interviewers through the Tangentyere Job Shop and conduct a training session for them on census day itself, Tuesday 7 August. Although I did not attend this training session, I did on that day have further contact with the census interviewer that I had observed in action the previous Thursday and Friday. He reported that he had 'not done all that much' as he had had a few personal issues to deal with. He had also clearly been somewhat discouraged by the experience of working on his own, as he suggested to me that it had been better working in a team, like he and the other interviewer and the CC had done on the Thursday morning. He intended checking in with the central Australian census manager in the next day or so, but was clearly finding the work pretty tough going.

The day after census day I met again with the central Australian census manager and a team of people from Tangentyere whom he had put together to do the homeless count in Alice Springs on census night. Although the team was drawn from Tangentyere, that night's work focused on places outside the 19 formally recognised town camps. It was intended to enumerate people who were sleeping rough that night, in places like the Todd River bed, which runs through the middle of Alice Springs and provides a convenient sitting place for Aboriginal people during the day and sometimes a sleeping place at night. This homeless enumeration appeared to have gone quite smoothly. It involved only a single short personal form with nine fairly straightforward questions (see Appendix D). So maintaining the interest and attention of numerous individuals over an extended period of time through both SIHFs and SIPFs was not an issue. For the interviewee, this was a quick, individualised one or two minute process, while for the interviewer it was simply a process of dealing quickly with one individual at a time and then moving on to find the next. The homeless persons census process enumerated 115 people in the Alice Springs area that night, all of whom identified themselves as Aboriginal.

While the central Australian census manager was clearly very pleased with the way the homeless persons census procedure had worked out, he was equally clearly quite worried about how the town camp enumeration procedure was going. He was aware that the original two interviewers had not done all that much and that the three he had trained on 7 August were only just getting going. He set about recruiting some more interviewers, including one who had helped with the homeless census and found it easy, and organising yet another training session, while also trying to provide some more support for the five interviewers and two CCs who were actually out there working.

On Thursday 9 August another training session was held for three new potential interviewers. Two were retained to the end of the training session and then taken into the camps under the supervision of the two CCs on Friday 10 August. Collection in the camps, with seven interviewers, continued over the weekend of 11–12 August and on 13 August a meeting was held at Tangentyere to see how they were all going. Some were clearly finding the work hard and were in danger of losing interest. A quick survey of the work that had been done produced the estimate that somewhat less than 100 people had actually been enumerated in the town camps in the 12 days since 2 August. There was still a long way to go. The collection effort in the town camps had been built up to the sort of level that the central Australian census manager had initially envisaged. But the census manager was still clearly worried that he was not going to be able to sustain the interest and effort of this group of interviewers and CCs for the two or three weeks that were still necessary for completing the collection in all the town camps. A decision point was looming.

The decision to focus on household forms

Largely by chance a discussion occurred on 13 August between the central Australian census manager and a senior member of the Tangentyere staff about how the census collection was progressing. As an observer who knew both these people, I was both privy to this discussion and a minor participant in it. It was quickly agreed that the current collection process was proving too arduous and was unlikely to be carried through to completion in the next two or three weeks. There was a danger of burning out the interviewers and the CCs, as well as the individuals being interviewed, before the task was done. A suggestion emerged: focusing first and foremost on the SIHFs would ensure that at least a basic enumeration would be completed.

The central Australian census manager decided to run this idea past his superior in Darwin. Within a couple of days a decision had been made, essentially to follow this course of action. Four columns were to be added manually to the SIHF for the recording of information relating to what Aboriginal language the person spoke, what the standard of their spoken English was, whether they were on CDEP, and whether they were of Aboriginal origin. Interviewers could then transfer these and the other basic data items from the enhanced SIHF to SIPFs in their own time away from the interviewees. This way the interviewers would be paid for the completion of the SIPFs, without the full SIPF process jeopardising the basic enumeration.

On Thursday 16 August another meeting was held at Tangentyere to see how things were going and to inform interviewers and CCs of this revised approach. Two interviewers had by this time fallen by the wayside due to the arduousness of the work, without having done much collecting. Two other interviewers had by the time of this meeting completed enumerations in a single town camp with which they were familiar, but were at this stage either unable or unwilling to take on further work. One of these was one of the two original interviewers, an older woman who was a senior resident of the town camp she had enumerated. She had worked diligently at the census collection task in this one town camp over a two-week period and now had other things to attend to in her life, including a funeral to organise. The other, a younger woman who did not live in the town camp she was enumerating, had informally recruited her father, a Tangentyere employee, to help her with the enumeration and together they had managed to do one camp in three days. But this was clearly more than enough for her.

So there were, in fact, only three interviewers who were available and willing to carry on collecting after this revised enumeration procedure had been devised. Yet the job at this stage was probably still less than half done. Two of these three remaining interviewers worked with one CC and one with the other. The team of three was quickly converted to the new collection procedure and conducted the census in three more town camps over the week of 17–24 August, filling out enhanced SIHFs in the camps and SIPFs elsewhere later. The lone interviewer working with the other CC was less keen on the idea of filling out forms away from people and so persisted with the original collection procedure during this week. He was, however, clearly a very competent collector with more stamina for the work than many of the others, so this was not necessarily a problem.

In the final week of 24–31 August, perhaps one-quarter of the census collection task in the Alice Springs town camps still remained to be done. But the two interviewers working with the one CC had by now had enough. One had domestic issues with which he had been dealing all along, which required him to move house, while the other simply lost interest. The two CCs and the one remaining interviewer all became interviewers and all began using the revised collection methodology. This was necessary just in order to get the job done by 31 August, when the actual census day on 7 August was for most people becoming a quite distant memory and the central Australian census manager was returning to Darwin.

The census collection in the Alice Springs town camps had, in essence, taken the whole of July to initiate and the whole of August to carry out. About 25 people had been suggested as possible interviewers, but only ten commenced training. Only seven completed training and commenced interviewing and only five lasted beyond the first few interviews, one of these only for three days and with the informal support and assistance of her father. A major change in procedure had been made half way through the collection period because only about 20 per cent of the work had by then been done. Even with this change in procedure, all but one of the interviewers was burnt out before the end of the process and the CCs were obliged to take on the role of interviewers just in order to get the job finished. Eventually about 980 people were enumerated in 190 dwellings in the Alice Springs town camps, over half of whom were enumerated using the revised collection procedure.

Analysis and policy implications for census collection

The foregoing account of the 2001 Census collection procedure in the Alice Springs town camps is fairly detailed because it raises some quite fundamental analytical issues for the IES, both as planned and as implemented. The implications for census collection policy in discrete Aboriginal communities like the Alice Springs town camps are quite profound and need to be discussed under a number of separate headings.

Demands and interest: the failure of the two-form structure

One major issue for analysis relates to how much the special enumeration strategy for the census demands of Aboriginal people as both interviewers and interviewees. The Alice Springs town camp experience in 2001 suggests that the strategy demands far too much of both interviewers and interviewees. The SIHF and SIPF structure is cumbersome and time consuming, and greatly extends the time that both interviewers and interviewees have to dedicate to the task. There is a constant danger that interviewers and interviewees will lose interest in the process before the enumeration is complete. People who have seen others being interviewed, or have other things to attend to, may not offer themselves for interview, while interviewers may burn out after doing just a few households.

To maintain the interest of both interviewers and interviewees the ABS probably needs to develop a simple single-form interview procedure which can be administered quickly. This single form structure could either be an enhanced household form, not unlike the one devised informally half way through the 2001 Alice Springs town camp enumeration process, or a simple personal form, not unlike the special short form used in the homeless enumeration (see Appendix D). The choice between these two single form structures would depend, to some extent, on whether the ABS sees the census as primarily concerned with enumerating and identifying the characteristics of individuals or of households. This is, of course, not entirely an either/or choice. A personal form could ask where people lived, how many other people lived there and whether the interviewee was related to those others, while a household form will inevitably collect some pieces of personal information. But it seems, on the basis of the Alice Springs town camp experience in 2001 that a personal form should be designed to be completed in no more than five minutes and a household form, for perhaps ten people, in no more than half to three-quarters of an hour. Otherwise momentum and interest—and people—will be lost.

Under the current two-form structure, by contrast, the enumeration of a household of ten can take up to two and a half hours, with people identified on the SIHF at the beginning expected to hang around for later completion of a SIPF. This is simply too much to ask and the count suffers as a result, through both interviewer burn out and interviewee avoidance.

Considerable thought would need to be given as to which single form structure, and associated personal or household collection emphasis, should be applied to discrete Aboriginal communities in sparsely settled northern and central Australia.

A worst-case scenario?

In the course of undertaking these observations, it was often suggested to me by the central Australian census manager that census collection in the Alice Springs town camps could, in many ways, be seen as something of a worst-case scenario. There is clearly a very high degree of mobility between the camps and the outlying Aboriginal communities. A good deal of drinking goes on in the camps, which makes collection difficult and at times unpleasant. The daily mobility of town camp residents out of the camps into other areas of Alice Springs is also a problem, making people hard to catch in the dwellings. The spread of the camps across town also makes travel to and from them, or between them, difficult for interviewers.

Despite all these worst-case characteristics, it seems to me that there are also aspects of the Alice Springs town camp situation that are very positive and helpful. Tangentyere is a well-established, cooperative, and able Indigenous organisation which cooperated well with the ABS. The interviewers recruited through Tangentyere's Job Shop and its general networks were also of high quality, being people who had through their past employment and other experience considerable exposure to non-Indigenous bureaucratic ways. On these latter counts, the situation in some remote Indigenous communities could be more challenging than in the Alice Springs town camps, with less well-established community organisations and less bureaucratically-experienced individuals on whom to draw as interviewers.

Usual residents or people present: who should be enumerated?

One further characteristic of the IES as implemented in the Alice Springs town camps was its emphasis on enumerating people who are usual residents of dwellings, plus visitors who were unlikely to be enumerated elsewhere. This is somewhat different from standard census practice, which is to enumerate people present on the night the census, plus absent usual residents who are unlikely to be enumerated elsewhere.

Formally, the IES strategy followed the standard census approach. This was reflected in the SIHF, which asked interviewers to list all people who live in the dwelling 'most of the time' including those who are 'away' and also all visitors. The SIHF then asked the interviewers to divide these people into those who needed a SIPF (i.e. to be enumerated here) and those who did not. And the accompanying training manual explained as follows:

All people need a Personal Form EXCEPT if they are away in a city, town, another community. If someone is away fishing, hunting, on sorry business, etc., you still need to complete a Personal Form for this person.

The emphasis here was on identifying absent usual residents who would be counted elsewhere and hence did not need to be counted here, to avoid double counting. But all people present, including visitors, were to be counted on SIPFs.

Informally, the Northern Territory census administration had tried to move more to a usual residents basis of enumeration, counting all usual residents including those absent. Visitors were only to be counted if it seemed likely that they would not be counted elsewhere as usual residents. In practice this seemed to mean that interviewers let visitors go, either not recording them at all, even on the SIHFs, or not filling in SIPFs for them.

This seemed to me a highly unsatisfactory resolution of the issue of who should be counted. People present were not being counted on the premise that they would be counted elsewhere as absent usual residents. However, this assumption seemed suspect on a number of counts. First, would they still be recognised as usual residents of a dwelling elsewhere, perhaps out in a bush community, if they had not been there for a while? Second, if they were recognised as absent usual residents somewhere else, would a SIPF be filled in for them? I had observed some willingness to put people not present on the list of household members for the SIHF, but a reluctance to fill in a SIPF for other than oneself. The personalised 'you' language of the SIPF seemed to encourage this reluctance. Third, and specifically in relation to the town camps, it was arguably just as important to count the population present as it was to count those who identified themselves as usual residents.

I would suggest that the Northern Territory census administration's attempt to move to a 'usual residents' basis for enumeration was somewhat half-baked and that in the Alice Springs town camps it probably allowed a lot of visitors, who might not in fact have been counted elsewhere, to slip through the census net. There seem to me to be very good arguments for sticking with the standard census procedure of enumerating people where census collectors encounter them, plus asking those present if there are other absent usual residents. Those present can be asked whether they are usual residents or visitors and if the latter, where their usual residence is. Those absent can be reasonably clearly divided into those who are likely to be enumerated elsewhere and those who are not. But visitors are extremely difficult to divide into those who are likely to be enumerated elsewhere and those who are not. To let the visitors go when they are encountered, on the assumption that others elsewhere will be asked about them and will answer for them, seems perverse. Surely the best source of information about a person is that person.

Time extension and the interview process: an underlying issue

The attempt by the Northern Territory census administration to move to a usual residents basis of enumeration for discrete Aboriginal communities is, I think, linked to the underlying issue of the time extension of census collection under the IES.

Standard census enumeration aims for a very short time extension to the count, enumerating people where they sleep on a single night. This can only really be accomplished if most of the count is done by self-enumeration. Where the count is done by interview, the time extension is inevitably going to be greater. Time extension, combined with mobility of the population, introduces a new source of possible counting error: missing people or encountering them more than once as they and the census collectors move around over time. Hence the drive towards identifying usual residents and discounting visitors. However, the significance of error due to time extension and mobility can be overstated. Error is reduced if one counts those present at the time of enumeration and asks, among other things, whether they have been counted elsewhere recently. There may still be under-enumeration due to missing some people altogether through mobility, but questions about absent usual residents can pick up on this too. Time extension does not need to entail a switch to a usual residents basis of enumeration. Enumeration can still be of those present, plus absent usual residents. The question that needs to be asked in a time extended census is not who slept in this dwelling on the night of 7 August or some other specific date, but who slept in this dwelling *last night*. In this way in a time extended census all dwellings get a census night, even if it is not quite the same census night as the dwelling next door or that in another community.

Individual questions: the issue of social relevance

In relation to individual questions, like those which caused concern for collectors and CCs in the initial training course, the following comments can be made. These all reflect, in one way or another, on what might be referred to as the social relevance of these questions to people living in discrete Aboriginal communities in sparsely settled northern and central Australia.

The attempt to get rent figures for houses from Tangentyere was unsuccessful. Although Tangentyere knew how much rent it collected in total from town camps, it did not allocate this rent definitively to individual houses. Tangentyere collects rent from individuals under a policy which is in fact more like an informal income tax regime, specifying that individuals with particular levels and types of employment and income will be required to contribute certain levels of payment. Some interviewers did obtain a rent figure for the dwellings they enumerated. How these relate to Tangentyere's rent policy and compare with its administrative figures for total rent collection will be interesting to see. The comparison may be a quite useful check on data quality, showing either that the information recorded accords generally with Tangentyere administrative records or that it is somewhat at odds with those records.

The age question did indeed often initially stop people in their tracks. But when rephrased in terms like 'well, in what year were you born?', it often then elicited an answer. I did however witness one miscalculation by ten years from the year of birth back to the actual age. So perhaps an ability to record the raw answer of the year of birth given may be useful. Or, as Morphy (this volume) suggests, an ability just to put people in five or ten year age groupings.

The income question appeared to cause no great problems, though there did seem to be little if any attention paid to the 'before tax' qualification. Figures quoted were most frequently fortnightly social security payment amounts, but were sometimes weekly CDEP pays which could be fairly easily doubled up and put into a broad income category.

Question 37 on the SIPF about whether the person had looked for work in the last four weeks did indeed often elicit the equivocation suggested. Some people were inclined to say 'no' at first, suggesting there wasn't any appropriate work around for them. But then they did wonder whether they were supposed to say 'yes', like on Newstart payment forms. In many ways the distinction between being unemployed and not being in the labour force, which this and subsequent questions try to construct, is of little if any social relevance in discrete Aboriginal communities in sparsely settled northern and central Australia. A person in these communities is either employed or they are not. So the line of questioning is a little bit socially irrelevant and nonsensical.

A couple of other questions which caused confusion also deserve to be commented on. Question 5 on the SIPF, the first that actually needed to be asked, caused confusion. It asked whether the person being interviewed was 'more closely related to anyone else here in this house' than person 1. The relationship between the person being interviewed and person 1 had been established in Q. 4—a question which did not in fact need to be answered, but had been information transferred from the SIHF. Clearly Q. 4 had to be revisited and the answer to it re-identified, if Q. 5 was to make any sense. However, even if this was done, Q. 5 still did not work very well, as there was not necessarily one single other person in the house to whom the person was more closely related. Is a spouse, a child, a parent, or a sibling one's closest relation? Or are they all contenders for that claim?

The question on ancestry (Q. 13) on the SIPF also confused people as it seemed in this context simply to repeat Q. 10 on Aboriginal or Torres Strait Islander origin. Question 10 itself was handled quite well, but like others where the answer was obvious, such as Q. 11 and Q. 12 on whether your mother and father were born in Australia, it was often handled in a joking manner. A joking approach to questions because of their obviousness was common, and was legitimated by the use of this technique in the training video for interviewers.

Question 23 on post-school education, as noted above, often elicited various responses about low level training courses which people had undertaken. This then tied people into answering four more questions about the name of the course, what it involved, the institution at which it was studied and the year it was completed. Whether this was the sort of information that these questions were intended to elicit, again raises the issue of the social relevance of some standard questions to the circumstances of Aboriginal Australians in discrete communities in sparsely settled northern and central Australia.

The Indigenous Enumeration Strategy: how special, how successful, how necessary?

I want to conclude this analysis by briefly addressing three related questions about the IES. How special, how successful and how necessary is it?

At one level, the IES does indeed seem quite special. It relies on interview rather than self-completion, on a separate two-form structure rather than the standard single household form and it is time extended, over a month rather than focused on a single day. However, the questions on the special Indigenous forms suggest a reluctance to move away from the standard questions and information sought on the standard household form. The standard household form and its standard questions seeking standard information have simply been broken up into a series of forms and questions with slightly more personalised language, asking in the SIPF about 'you' rather than 'the person' and dealing with each person individually for each question rather than all people in the household together for each question as in the standard household form.

This is arguably a 'worst of both worlds' solution to the challenge of devising an appropriate census collection methodology for Indigenous Australians in discrete communities in sparsely settled northern and central Australia. The content of the census remains standard, but the collection process actually becomes more complex and elaborate. Interviewers are asked to coordinate SIHFs and SIPFs through person numbers, as well as record numbers, and to transfer items of information between SIHFs and SIPFs. Interviewees are asked to hang around during a two-form, two-stage drawn out interview process and to revisit bits of information already elicited. The 'you' language of the SIPF also actually discourages people from filling out forms for others, even though the push to enumerate people on a usual residents basis in the Northern Territory in fact relies on lots of people filling out SIPFs for absent others.

So I am not, in fact, convinced that in the Alice Springs town camps in 2001 at least, the IES was very successful at all. Indeed, it had to be modified half way through just in order to get a basic enumeration completed. In many ways it seemed that the special enumeration only improved on the standard enumeration in two respects—in being time-extended and interview-based. Another way of putting this would be to say that the 2001 Census might have been just as easily and successfully carried out in the Alice Springs town camps by sending in the interviewers armed with standard census household forms with two slight modifying instructions: enumerate all people who spent the night at the dwelling the previous night (rather than on 7 August), and complete multiple household forms for the one dwelling if there are more than six people present. What would have been 'special' about the Indigenous enumeration would have then simply been that it was time-extended and interview-based. But it would have been a much more standard census procedure in being an enumeration of people present, first and foremost, combined with the subsequent identification of absent usual residents. And it would have also been easier for people to fill in forms for others, as there would not have been identifiable SIPFs, with their personalised 'you' language.

This is perhaps a harsh judgment on the success of and need for the IES. But it is, to my mind, worth considering, if only in thinking seriously about how best to proceed in the future and what elements of the IES are indeed necessary, and which are unnecessary complications.

The alternative to reverting to a far more standardised census collection procedure, adapted only by time extension and interview processes, would seem to be to go for a far more thoroughly thought-through Indigenous enumeration process, with as much emphasis on changes in the content of what is asked as on changes in the process through which people are enumerated and information is collected. But even if such a more thoroughly thought-through strategy were developed, I would argue strongly against any shift away from the standard census procedures of enumerating people where they are presently sleeping, rather than where they are usual residents. Enumerating those present stands as something of a bedrock principle for census administration. It is surely the most reliable way to count people and to find out from them, directly, their basic demographic and socioeconomic characteristics. When combined with sensible questioning about absent usual residents and, because of time extension, questioning about whether a person has been counted before recently, it surely provides still the best way to enumerate any population, no matter how mobile or how different its circumstances from broader community norms.

5. The Indigenous Enumeration Strategy: an overview assessment and ideas for improvement

David Martin, Frances Morphy, Will Sanders and John Taylor

This brief final chapter offers both an overview assessment of the conduct of the 2001 Census, based on a synthesis of the case studies, and some ideas for future improvement of the ABS's Indigenous Enumeration Strategy, as applied to Aboriginal communities in sparsely settled northern and central Australia. The chapter is in three parts entitled 'Who to count', 'How to count' and 'What to ask'. These seem to us to address the big issues that arise from the case studies and also to cover the ways in which the census could perhaps be better adapted to the circumstances of Aboriginal people in northern and central Australia in the future.

Who to count

The standard census procedure in Australia is to count those who sleep in each dwelling on census night, asking them whether they are usual residents or visitors and also asking them whether there are other absent usual residents of the dwelling. In the IES this is still, officially, the approach. However, in the Northern Territory, where two of our case studies were located, there is some tendency to move towards a 'usual residents' basis of counting. In this approach, all usual residents of a dwelling are counted and visitors to a dwelling are not counted if they have some other usual residence where it is judged they will be counted. We say some 'tendency', since this only occurred in one of our two Northern Territory case studies.

The counting in Morphy's outstation case study was, in our judgment, essentially done using the standard procedure of counting those in situ and asking them about absent usual residents. This procedure carries some potential for double counting, if absent usual residents are also counted elsewhere as visitors. But the in situ principle has the advantage of counting people where they are found, or 'encountered', and of relying on the people themselves for information about their demographic and socioeconomic characteristics. The reasons that the Northern Territory branch of the ABS seems tempted to abandon this methodology in favour of a usual residents count would appear to relate to the time extension involved in the IES and to Indigenous people's high levels of residential mobility. Because the IES is interview-based, it takes a week or weeks, rather than a day or two, and is often occurring in different places at different times. The Northern Territory administration of the ABS fears that through this time extension and with people's mobility, counting in situ will miss people, as both they and the census collectors move around. While under-counting *is* a possible outcome of time extension and mobility, we do not believe that switching to a usual residents basis of counting solves this problem. We also believe that such a strategy introduces problems of its own, relating potentially to both under-counting and to data quality.

In the Alice Springs town camps, for example, where the usual residents method of counting was used, a number of people who were present in the town camps at the time of the census were not counted, on the grounds that that they were only visitors and would be counted elsewhere as usual residents. But the point has been made in all the case studies that Aboriginal people in northern and central Australia often move between several dwellings within one or more than one community location and so it is not clear that all such visitors will in fact be counted elsewhere as usual residents of a particular dwelling. Indeed, as the case studies and earlier work by Martin and Taylor (1995) show, people can be missed even when their mobility is only within one community between several dwellings. The idea of counting usual residents is too much of a gamble and it also means that more census interviewees are supplying information about third parties, which introduces greater data quality concerns. The methodology used in the Alice Springs town camps probably led to a greater under-count than that used in the Northern Territory outstation case study. While the number of usual residents of the town camps was probably reasonably well captured, the number of visitors in the town camps at the time of the census was not well captured at all. It is quite possible that not counting these people in the town camps contributed to under-counts in the larger central Australian region, as they were possibly not counted elsewhere.

The Aurukun case study in far north Queensland, along with the outstation case study in the Northern Territory, shows how counting those present, plus asking them about absent usual residents, can work as a census methodology in Aboriginal communities. As we have suggested, this methodology will, if anything, err towards double counting; however, this would seem the lesser of two evils and can at least potentially be eliminated by informed cross-checking between areas. No such cross-checking is even potentially possible when visitors encountered in particular places are not counted, on the assumption that they will counted elsewhere as usual residents.[1]

The other way to guard against both double-counting and under-counting using the standard census methodology is to specify more clearly the treatment of absent usual residents. Presently the training package specifies that people who are 'away fishing, hunting, on sorry business, etc.' should have a SIPF filled out for them and hence be counted, as it is judged that they are unlikely to be counted elsewhere. It also specifies that if they are 'away in a city, town or other community' they do not need a SIPF because it is judged likely they will be counted elsewhere. This seems to us too generous an assumption. Two of our case studies identified the issue of usual residents away at sports carnivals in Aboriginal communities. In both cases there was no attempt made to count those at the sports carnival, and indeed at Yuendumu there was a deliberate choice made to move the count away from the carnival. So under the standard census counting methodology these people need to be put clearly in the category of absent usual residents who need to be counted at their usual residence, which in the two-form structure means having a SIPF completed in their absence. Sports carnivals constitute one very important case in which the circumstances of absent usual residents from Indigenous communities need to be more closely specified, but probably not the only one.

The standard ABS approach to the issue of who to count, advocated by both central office and all State and Territory administrations within the ABS except the Northern Territory, needs in our view to be adhered to. It is not perfect, but it is the best available resolution of the issue, particularly if the circumstances in which to count absent usual residents are well elaborated. To keep error due to time extension to a minimum, the best solution is simply to keep time extension of the count itself to a minimum. This may be achieved, in part, by streamlining the interview procedures, which is an issue relevant to both of our next two sections.

How to count

The IES, as currently practiced in northern and central Australia, relies on two major adaptations in how the count proceeds: an interview process, rather than household self-completion of a form, and a modified household plus personal form structure. While the interview process seems to us to be indispensable and working well as an adaptation, we do not believe that the two-form structure is working well at all. The two- or three-form structure—if we count the community-level Dwelling Check List as well—is administratively cumbersome and far too demanding on both Aboriginal interviewers and interviewees. The structure only worked in the Aurukun and outstation case studies which we observed because the SIHFs were largely filled out beforehand away from interviewees. But even in these cases, filling out just the SIPFs with interviewees was a time-consuming and onerous task which tested the endurance and interest of both the interviewers and the interviewees to the limit. In the Alice Springs case study, where an attempt was made to fill out both the SIHFs and SIPFs in the presence of interviewees, this proved far too demanding and cumbersome and had to be abandoned.

We believe that for Aboriginal communities in northern and central Australia it should be possible to design a single household form that can be administered by interview. This form should build on the existing SIHF, with its provision for large numbers of people in a household, and it should extend the numbers of questions asked of individuals on that form beyond the basic age, sex, usual resident/visitor demographics. Such a form would be a move towards the more standard census household form structure, and an argument could even be made that the appropriate adaptation is to do interviews using standard household forms in some Indigenous communities. But for the more traditionally-oriented communities in northern and central Australia with low levels of western economic activity and in which English is often not the first language of spoken daily interaction, we believe that there is a need for a specific, restricted Indigenous household form.

If we recall, from Chapter 1, the way in which the IES started as an adaptation of the census to the circumstances of more traditionally-oriented Aboriginal communities in the Northern Territory and Western Australia in 1976 and 1981, before spreading to South Australia, Queensland and, in 2001, also into New South Wales, we can perhaps see where it has gone somewhat astray. Its ability to focus specifically on the circumstances of more traditionally-oriented Aboriginal communities in northern and central Australia has probably been somewhat weakened over the years, while it has probably also been somewhat unnecessarily applied in places like New South Wales where many people living in discrete Aboriginal communities could probably deal with standard census forms and with household self-completion of forms.

Our solution would be to distinguish the interview from the 'special form' aspect of census adaptation. While both could be used in the most traditionally-oriented Aboriginal communities, like those in our case studies, interviews with standard forms could be used in other Aboriginal communities. This would make it possible to design the new Indigenous household form specifically for the circumstances of the most traditionally-oriented Aboriginal communities in northern and central Australia. Some Indigenous communities might also have mixtures of households who used the standard and special household forms with and without interview. This leads us on the issue of what questions should be asked in this revised Indigenous household form.

What to ask

This is the most difficult issue of all. While many standard questions seem of little social relevance to circumstances in traditionally-oriented communities, and produce answers which are close to nonsensical, we also acknowledge that there are enormous political and social pressures for the retention of standard questions so that an attempt can be made to construct standard statistics comparing Indigenous and other Australians.

We believe, nevertheless, that it is possible to devise a simplified Indigenous household form that is tailored more precisely to the circumstances of traditionally-oriented Indigenous people. The general principles which should motivate its design and content are:

• that as a first step, the information to be sought should be ranked in order of priority, and the form should concentrate on eliciting the most important data;

• that the number of questions should be reduced to the necessary minimum;

• that pathways through the form should be as streamlined as possible;

• that the questions should be grounded in the realities of Indigenous lifestyles;

• but designed so that the data outcomes ensure commensurability with data from the mainstream count.

These principles will be briefly exemplified through a consideration of the questions on household composition and structure, place (of residence or of work), origin and ancestry, labour force statistics, education, and culture (as indicated by the questions on language and religion). Other, more detailed recommendations are to be found in the individual chapters.

Household composition and structure

The census cannot hope to capture the complexity of Indigenous principles of kinship and household structure. The attempt to do so in the 2001 Census led to the collection of incoherent and uninterpretable data (see in particular the case studies by Martin and Morphy). The further step of 'classifying' this data into the family types recognised in ABS definitions, which do not coincide with the family types found in many, if not most, Indigenous communities, is a completely spurious exercise, and any analysis which takes these data as a basis must allow for this. It should be noted that the complex familial structures of Indigenous societies are one of their most enduring aspects, persisting in communities in 'settled' Australia as well as in remote, 'traditionally-oriented' communities (see Smith 2000b).

The designers of the census need to step back from the questions on household structure, and decide precisely *what* information they wish to elicit. Is it information primarily about family structure, or about the age distribution, gender composition, and dependency structures of households? [2] If it is decided that the latter data are the most important, one possibility which would sit more comfortably with the Indigenous facts would be to add a new type of household to the ABS list—the *extended family household*. This definition would apply to large households in which everyone is related to everyone else, and would therefore conflate the 'family' with the usual residents of the dwelling, or household. It would not attempt to distinguish any putative 'couple families' or 'one-parent' families among the residents of the dwelling, and the post-enumeration categorisation would not attempt to break extended family households into such smaller family units.

This solution is grounded in Indigenous reality, in that it recognises the incommensurability of Indigenous and mainstream principles of household formation (as defined currently by the ABS), while still allowing the dwelling to function as a unit of analysis and measurement across the board. It does not address the issue of linked households, which are such a prevalent feature of Indigenous community life, but that problem seems insoluble given the dwelling-based framework of the census enumeration.

Place

If place were defined to refer unambiguously to the community in question rather than to an address within the community, this would eliminate the need to provide numerous instances of 'addresses', identified by Morphy as both unduly time-consuming and culturally inappropriate. It would also circumvent the problem, highlighted by Martin, of identifying place of residence over time in communities where there is both a high level of intra-community mobility and a high turnover of housing stock.

Ancestry and origin

The set of questions on ancestry and origin should be framed from the Indigenous perspective, not from that of the settler culture. If all that is required is an 'Indigenous identifier' (as the case in most Australian census enumerations), then only one question needs to be asked, and that is: 'Are you of Aboriginal or Torres Strait Islander origin?'.

The questions on overseas parentage are almost certainly superfluous in the vast majority of cases. If more detailed information on ethnicity is sought in future censuses, then the supplementary question should be framed in terms of non-Indigeneity, and the prompts should include 'non-Indigenous Australian', the main Anglo-Celtic categories, Chinese and Afghan, all of which are more likely ancestries for Indigenous Australians than some of the ones suggested in the prompt to the question on the 2001 SIPF.

Education

In many cases, neither the interviewers nor the interviewees will have a high level of formal education. In whichever way the questions on education are framed, the Indigenous interviewers need focused training on the precise meanings of the questions, and on how to interpret the likely answers of the respondents. This applies particularly to the question of further education, where interviewers need clear guidance on what counts as an accredited course, and what is meant by 'full name' and 'field of study'. They should also be helped to identify what counts as a 'place of study'.

Work

The vast majority of Indigenous people in the north and centre of Australia live in areas where there is very little employment, in the mainstream sense of the word. 'Looking for work', in this context, is a pointless activity for most people. In the 2001 Census, the series of questions on the SIPF on employment and looking for work were constructed on the premise that labour market conditions in these regions are comparable to those in other parts of Australia. CDEP schemes were treated as if their sole purpose is to provide 'real' jobs, and all CDEP participants were deemed to have a job. The design of the questions rested, therefore, on two fictions: firstly that there is a local labour market in which employment can be sought, and secondly that all CDEP participants are in paid employment.

This is another example of the dilemma faced in trying to reconcile local Indigenous reality with comparability across the board. For many reasons, comparability may be considered a desirable outcome, and one which outweighs other considerations. That is the first question to be settled. If the principle of comparability is to be preserved, some thought needs to be given as to how the level, or degree of fiction can be reduced, both in the forms of the questions and in the likely responses.

The limits to quantifiability

If the quantifiable population characteristics of Indigenous Australians are to emerge clearly from census data, the questions on the Indigenous form need to be as culturally neutral as possible, in order to minimise misunderstanding on the part of the Indigenous interviewers and respondents. If a person fails to understand the meaning of a question, they are unlikely to provide the kind of answer that is sought. Care must be taken to avoid the 'naturalisation' of Anglo-Celtic cultural categories and assumptions, as happened with the 'nuclear family' and with the 'ethnic' division of the Australian population in the questions on ancestry and origin. We would further suggest that, given the increasing ethnic diversity of the Australian population, this issue may not be unique to Indigenous people.

That being said, the case studies by Martin and Morphy show clearly that certain kinds of questions, however they are phrased, particularly those that address core elements of contemporary Indigenous identity, are likely to elicit answers that are symbolic rather than technical (in Martin's terminology). The responses to the question on religion are a case in point. The design of the question itself played a part, in making the equation between 'Traditional Beliefs' and Christian denominations, and in failing to signal clearly that more than one answer was possible. It is interesting that the responses in both communities were symbolic, but they were different. In Aurukun, there was perhaps a symbolic identification of 'Traditional Beliefs' with a private Wik domain, not considered appropriate for exposure in a non-Indigenous context, whereas in the outstation community (but not elsewhere in the region, it must be noted) 'Traditional Beliefs' were embraced as a public symbol of Aboriginality. The question on the ability to speak English elicited a symbolic answer from Wik respondents, because of the connection that they make between lack of English and 'being myall', but in the Northern Territory outstation, where the ability to speak English is viewed merely as a useful skill, the answers were technical in nature.

Some questions are inherently more likely than others to elicit symbolic replies. Such responses, which are indicative of underlying beliefs and attitudes rather than constituting objective answers to factual questions, are not amenable to quantitative analysis.

Conclusion

We believe that the five-yearly national census can be better adapted to the circumstances of traditionally-oriented Aboriginal people in northern and central Australia than was the case, as we observed it, in 2001. Adaptation is not a simple task and all methodologies will have their weaknesses and pitfalls. The ABS is to be commended for its openness in allowing us to observe and to constructively criticise its operations in 2001. Interaction between the ABS and academic researchers should be an ongoing relationship in which ideas for improvement of the census methodology for more traditionally-oriented Aboriginal people in northern and central Australia are continually put to the test. This could of course be a more chastening experience for the researchers than for the ABS. Reckoning the Indigenous people of the Commonwealth will never be an easy task.

Notes

1. To be fair, the official approach in the Alice Springs town camps was that visitors who would be counted elsewhere as usual residents should be recorded on SIHFs but not required to fill out SIPFs. However, as we saw in that case study, in the face of a demanding task, this quickly became interpreted as a reason not record them on either type of form.

2. This exercise might be worth undertaking for the census in its entirety, and not just the Indigenous enumeration, since members of many of Australia's other 'ethnic' communities also likely to live in households that diverge in their structure from the types envisaged in the present ABS definitions. It is perhaps time to consider retreating from the 'nuclear family' as the model against which *all* household structures are measured, not just Indigenous households.

Appendix A. Dwelling Check List, 2001 Census

			Dwelling Check List				
Australian Bureau of Statistics	**census** 7 August 2001			**CD Number** **State** ☐☐☐ ☐☐☐☐☐			

Interviewer

Community/outstation/location   **Postcode**

Record Number	Name of Family	Address/Description of place	Tick when complete	Personal forms completed			Comments
				Male	Female	Total	

Sample only

	Ticks	Male	Female	Total
15 *Add up each column and print numbers here*				

Appendix B. Special Indigenous Household Form, 2001 Census

Special Indigenous Household Form

Australian Bureau of Statistics

7 August 2001

census

Record No. (RNO)

Why a Census?

The Census is a count of everyone in Australia. It is the only practical way to get information on how many people there are in each part of Australia, what they do and how they live. This information will help in planning services like schools, hospitals and housing.

Collection authority

The information asked for is collected under the authority of the *Census and Statistics Act 1905*. Your co-operation is sought in completing this form.

Confidentiality

Under the *Census and Statistics Act*, the ABS must not release any information you provide in a way which would enable an individual's or household's data to be identified. The one exception is if a person agrees at Question 39 on the Personal Form, then that person's information will be provided to the National Archives of Australia for release in 99 years time.

How to complete the form

Please use a **black or blue pen.**

Most questions only need to be answered by **marking a box** like this, ☞ —

or writing a number like this. ☞ 3 2 1

Please use **BLOCK** letters, and ☞ A U S T R A L I A

write like this, keeping each letter within the boxes provided. ☞ Y O U R   C O M M U N I T Y

Please answer **all** the questions unless the form asks you not to.

If you **do not know** an answer, give the best answer you can.

If a mistake is made, cross out the answer and give the correct answer.

Please do not fold or bend this form.

Name of family

Address/Description of place

Community/outstation/location　　　　　　　　　**Postcode**

} Copy from Dwelling Check List

List of all people who live here and people who are staying here

Person Number	Name: • List people in family groups • Include all children and babies • Include all people who live here most of the time, but are away.	Sex Write 'M' or 'F'	Age	How is this person related to Person 1? (Head of house)	If visitor write 'V'	Personal Form Needed? Yes/No
1				Person 1		
2						
3						
4						
5						
6						
7						
8						
9						
10						
11						
12						
13						
14						
15						
16						
17						
18						
19						
20						
21						
22						
23						
24						
25						
26						
27						
28						
29						
30						
31						
32						
33						
34						
35						

Sample only

1 Is this place occupied?
(Interviewer to answer)

- Yes
- No ► Answer question 2 only

2 Is this place a house?
(Interviewer to answer)

- Yes
- No – caravan, tin shed or cabin
- No – humpy, tent or sleepout ► Go to 7

3 How many bedrooms are there in this place?

[ ][ ] Number of bedrooms

4 What is the total amount being paid for this place each week?

- Exclude electricity, repairs, council rates etc.
- If no payments, please mark 'NIL' box.

$ [ ][ ][ ][ ] . 0 0 per week

- NIL

5 Is this place being rented?

- Yes, rented
- No, being bought ► Go to 7
- No, owned ► Go to 7
- No, being occupied rent-free
- No, other ► Go to 7

6 Who is the place rented from?

- Community or co-operative housing group
- Government Housing Authority
- Employer – Government
- Employer – Private
- Other

7 How many registered vehicles were parked at this place last night?

- Please mark both sets of boxes.
- If none, write '0'.

[ ][ ] Motor vehicles

[ ][ ] Motorbikes and motor scooters

Field Use Only

CD Number

State
[ ][ ][ ] [ ][ ][ ][ ][ ]

Record No. (RNO)

0	0	0	0
1	1	1	1
2	2	2	2
3	3	3	3
4	4	4	4
5	5	5	5
6	6	6	6
7	7	7	7
8	8	8	8
9	9	9	9

Number of Personal Forms Completed

Males			Females		
0	0	0	0	0	0
1	1	1	1	1	1
2	2	2	2	2	2
3	3	3	3	3	3
4	4	4	4	4	4
	5	5		5	5
	6	6		6	6
	7	7		7	7
	8	8		8	8
	9	9		9	9

Office Use Only

TF

[ ] 1

Sample only

Appendix C. Special Indigenous Personal Form, 2001 Census

Special Indigenous Personal Form

Record No. (RNO)

Person No. (PNO)

Why a Census?

The Census is a count of everyone in Australia. It is the only practical way to get information on how many people there are in each part of Australia, what they do and how they live. This information will help in planning services like schools, hospitals and housing.

Collection authority

The information asked for is collected under the authority of the *Census and Statistics Act 1905*. Your co-operation is sought in completing this form.

Confidentiality

Under the *Census and Statistics Act*, the ABS must not release any information which would enable an individual's data to be identified. The one exception is if you agree at Question 39 then your information will be provided to the National Archives of Australia for release in 99 years time.

How to complete the form

Please use a **black or blue pen.**

Most questions only need to be answered by **marking a box** like this, ☞ —

or writing a number like this. ☞ `3` `2` `1`

Please use **BLOCK** letters, and ☞ `A` `U` `S` `T` `R` `A` `L` `I` `A`

write like this, keeping each letter within the boxes provided. ☞ `Y` `O` `U` `R` ` ` `C` `O` `M` `M` `U` `N` `I` `T` `Y`

Please answer **all** the questions unless the form asks you not to.

If you **do not know** an answer, give the best answer you can.

If a mistake is made, cross out the answer and give the correct answer.

Please do not fold or bend this form.

Interviewer Note: Copy the answers to Questions 1, 2, 3 and 4 from page 2 of the Household Form.

1　What is your name?

First name

Surname or family name

2　Sex:

Mark one box, for example ▬ .

☐ Male

☐ Female

3　How old are you?

If age is less than one year, write '0'.

☐☐ Years

☐ 100 years or more

4　How are you related to Person 1 (Head of house)?

Examples of relationships: husband, wife, de facto partner, son, daughter, granddaughter, uncle, son-in-law, friend, unrelated.

☐ Person 1

Relationship to Person 1

5　Are you more closely related to anyone else here in this house?

☐ No

☐ Yes, who?

Name

Relationship e.g. grandson, niece, daughter

6　Are you married?

Prompt categories below.

☐ Never married

☐ Widowed

☐ Divorced

☐ Separated but not divorced

☐ Married

7　Do you live at this place most of the time?

☐ Yes, at this place

☐ No, somewhere else – please write address

Street number

Street name

Suburb, rural locality or town

State/Territory　　　　Postcode

8　Did you live at this place most of the time one year ago?

Ask: last dry season.

If the person is less than one year old, leave blank.

☐ Same as in question 7

☐ No, somewhere else – please write address

Street number

Street name

Suburb, rural locality or town

State/Territory　　　　Postcode

9　Did you live at this place most of the time five years ago?

Ask: dry season, last Census.

If the person is less than five years old, leave blank.

☐ Same as in question 7

☐ Same as in question 8

☐ No, somewhere else – please write address

Street number

Street name

Suburb, rural locality or town

State/Territory　　　　Postcode

Sample only

10 Are you of Aboriginal or Torres Strait Islander origin?

- For persons of both Aboriginal and Torres Strait Islander origin, mark both 'Yes' boxes.

　No

　Yes, Aboriginal

　Yes, Torres Strait Islander

11 Was your father born in Australia?

　Yes, Australia

　No, other country

12 Was your mother born in Australia?

　Yes, Australia

　No, other country

13 What is your ancestry?

- For example, Vietnamese, Hmong, Dutch, Kurdish, Australian South Sea Islander, Maori, Lebanese.
- Provide more than one ancestry if necessary.

　Aboriginal

　Torres Strait Islander

　Other – please specify

14 Do you speak an Aboriginal or Torres Strait Islander language *at home*?

- If Aboriginal or Torres Strait Islander language, please give the name of the language.
- If more than one language, indicate the one that is spoken most often.

　No, speaks only English ▶ Go to 16

　Yes – please write language

15 How well do you speak *English*?

　Very well

　Well

　Not well

　Not at all

16 What is your religion?

- Answering this question is **OPTIONAL**.
- If no religion, mark last box.

　Anglican (Church of England)

　Catholic

　Uniting Church

　Lutheran

　Baptist

　Traditional Beliefs

　Aboriginal Evangelical Missions

　Other – please specify

　No religion

17 Did you use a personal computer at home last week?

　No

　Yes

18 Did you use the Internet anywhere last week?

- Mark all applicable boxes.

　No

　Yes, at home

　Yes, at work

　Yes, elsewhere

19 Do you go to school, TAFE or university?

- Include school of the air, external or correspondence students.

　No ▶ Go to 21

　Yes, full-time student

　Yes, part-time student

20 What type of school or place of education do you go to?

- Include school of the air, external or correspondence students.

　Pre-school

Infants/Primary school

　Government

　Catholic

　Other non-government

Secondary school

　Government

　Catholic

　Other non-government

Tertiary institution

　Technical or further educational institution (including TAFE Colleges)

　University or other higher educational institution

　Other educational institution

Sample only

21 Are you 15 years of age or more?

- No, under 15 years ▶ **Go to 39**
- Yes, 15 years or more

22 What is the highest level of primary or secondary school you have completed?

- Mark one box only.
- For persons who returned after a break to complete their schooling, mark the highest level completed when they last left.

- Still at school
- Did not go to school
- Year 8 or below
- Year 9 or equivalent
- Year 10 or equivalent
- Year 11 or equivalent
- Year 12 or equivalent

23 Have you *finished* a trade certificate/apprenticeship, TAFE course or university course since leaving school?

- No ▶ **Go to 28**
- No, still studying for first course ▶ **Go to 28**
- Yes, trade certificate/apprenticeship
- Yes, other course

24 What is the name of that course?

- If more than one course, ask for the name of the highest level course.
- For example, trade certificate, bachelor degree, associate diploma.

Full name of course

25 What did you study?

- For example, plumbing, primary school teaching.

Field of study

26 What was the name of the place you studied at?

- Include external and correspondence institutions.

Name of place

27 In which year did you *finish* that course?

Year course finished

28 How much money do you get each *fortnight* before tax?

- Mark one box only.
- A fortnight is two weeks.
- Include salary, government payments, CDEP money, other money, before tax or anything else is taken out.

- $1,200 or more per fortnight
- $1,000 - $1,199 per fortnight
- $800 - $999 per fortnight
- $600 - $799 per fortnight
- $400 - $599 per fortnight
- $320 - $399 per fortnight
- $240 - $319 per fornight
- $160 - $239 per fortnight
- $80 - $159 per fortnight
- $1 - $79 per fortnight
- Nil income
- Negative income

29 Did you have a paid job *last week*?

- Mark one box only.
- A job means any type of work including casual or temporary work or part-time work, if it was for one hour or more.

- Yes, worked – CDEP
- Yes, worked other than CDEP
- Yes, worked in own business
- Yes, but off work on holiday, sick leave, sorry business.
- No, did not have a job ▶ **Go to 37**

30 What job did you do *last week*?

- For example, cleaner, council labourer, truck driver, station hand.

Name of job

31 What things did you do in that job *last week*?

- For example, cleaning school, mowing lawns, rubbish collection, mustering cattle.

Type of job

32 Who did you work for *last week*?

- If it is the community, give the community's name.
- If funded by CDEP, also write 'CDEP'.
- If they worked for themselves, write name of business.

Name of business

Sample only

33 What is your workplace address?

Street number

Street name

Community, rural locality or town

State/Territory   Postcode

34 What work does your employer do?

- For example, raising cattle, community services, community council, mining.
- If worked for CDEP write 'community council'.

35 How many hours did you work *last week*?

- Do not include any time off. Include any overtime or extra time worked.

☐ None

☐☐ Hours worked

36 How do you get to work?

- If the person used more than one method of travel to work, **mark all methods** used.

☐ Car – as driver
☐ Car – as passenger
☐ Bus
☐ Truck
☐ Motorbike or motor scooter
☐ Bicycle
☐ Walked only
☐ Worked at home
☐ Other
☐ Did not go to work

37 Did you look for work at any time in the *last four weeks*?

- Examples of actively looking for work include: being registered with Centrelink as a job seeker; checking or registering with any other employment agency; writing, telephoning or applying in person to an employer for work; or advertising for work.

☐ No, did not look for work ▶ **Go to 39**
☐ Yes, looked for full-time work
☐ Yes, looked for part-time work

38 If you had found a job, could you have started work *last week*?

☐ Yes, could have started work last week
☐ No, already had a job to go to
☐ No, temporarily ill or injured
☐ No, other reason

39 Do you agree to your name and address and other information on this form being kept by the National Archives of Australia and then made publicly available after 99 years?

- Answering this question is **OPTIONAL**.
- A person's name identified information will not be kept where a person does not agree or the answer is left blank.

☐ Yes, agrees
☐ No, does not agree

40 Declaration

I interviewed the person named at question 1 and explained the requirements of question 39 to the person. I believe the person understood my explanation of question 39 and that I have correctly recorded the person's views at question 39.

Signature of interviewer

Date

Thank you for completing this form.
Australian Statistician

Sample only

Field Use Only

CD Number

State

Record No. (RNO)

0	0	0	0
1	1	1	1
2	2	2	2
3	3	3	3
4	4	4	4
5	5	5	5
6	6	6	6
7	7	7	7
8	8	8	8
9	9	9	9

Person
No. (PNO)

0	0	0
1	1	1
2	2	2
3	3	3
4	4	4
	5	5
	6	6
	7	7
	8	8
	9	9

Office Use Only

TF

1

Sample only

Appendix D. Special Short Form, 2001 Census

Australian Bureau of Statistics

7 August 2001

census

Special Short Form

When should a Special Short Form be used?

A Special Short Form should be used for anyone who is sleeping out, or staying in a squat or improvised dwelling and who is unlikely to be completing a Personal Census form at a hostel, refuge or other accommodation.

---

1   **Have you already completed a census form, or are you likely to be completing a census form later tonight? (If Yes, <u>do not</u> ask any further questions).**

    (   )   Yes   ►   **No more questions**

    (   )   No   ►   **Go to 2**

2   **Is this person male or female?**

    (   )   Male   (   )   Female

3   **What was your age last birthday?**

    [   ]   Years

4   **Are you of Aboriginal or Torres Strait Islander origin?**

    • For persons of both Aboriginal and Torres Strait Islander origin, mark both 'Yes' boxes.

    (   )   No

    (   )   Yes, Aboriginal

    (   )   Yes, Torres Strait Islander

5   **What is your present marital status?**

    (   )   Never Married

    (   )   Widowed

    (   )   Divorced

    (   )   Separated but not divorced

    (   )   Married

6   **What is your weekly income from all sources?**

    (   ) $160 - $199 per week (Newstart Allowance)

    (   ) $1 - $159 per week

    (   )   Nil income

7   **Do you agree to your name and other information on this form being kept by the National Archives of Australia and then made publicly available after 99 years?**

    • Answering this question is **OPTIONAL**.

    (   )   Yes, agrees   ►   **Go to 8**

    (   )   No, does not agree   ►   **No more questions**

8 **Name of this person.**

First or given name

Surname or family name

9 **Declaration**

- Signature only required if an answer is provided for question 7.

I interviewed the person named at question 8 and explained the requirements of question 7 to the person. I believe the person understood my explanation of question 7 and that I have correctly recorded the person's views at question 7.

Signature

Date

Collector's Use Only

CD Number

State

Record No. (RNO)

Street name

Suburb

Location eg. soup kitchen, shelter.

Sample only

References

Aboriginal and Torres Strait Islander Commission (ATSIC) Tasmania 2000. Submission No. IFI/SUB/0041, Commonwealth Grants Commission (CGC) Indigenous Funding Inquiry, CGC, Canberra.

Altman, J.C. 1987. *Hunter-Gatherers Today: An Aboriginal Economy in North Australia,* Australian Institute of Aboriginal Studies, Canberra.

Anderson, J.C. 1982. 'The Bloomfield community, north Queensland', in E.A. Young and E.K. Fisk (eds), *Small Rural Communities*, Development Studies Centre, ANU, Canberra.

Australian Bureau of Statistics (ABS) 1989. *Census 86: Data Quality Aboriginal and Torres Strait Islander Counts*, Cat. no. 2602.0, ABS, Canberra.

— 1991. *Working for the Census*, ABS, Canberra.

— 1993. '1991 Census data quality: Aboriginal and Torres Strait Islander counts', *Census Working Paper No. 93/6*, ABS, Canberra.

— 1998. *Experimental Estimates of the Aboriginal and Torres Strait Islander Population,* Cat. no. 3230.0, ABS, Canberra.

— 2001. *2001 Census Dictionary* [http://www.abs.gov.au].

— 2002. *Population Distribution: Aboriginal and Torres Strait Islander Australians, 2001*, Cat. no. 4705.0, ABS, Canberra.

Benham, D. and Howe, A. 1994. 'Experimental estimates of the Aboriginal and Torres Strait Islander population 1986–1991: States/Territories and Australia', *Demography Working Paper No. 94/2*, ABS, Canberra.

Choi, C. and Gray, A. 1985. 'An evaluation of census counts of the Aboriginal population, 1971, 1976 and 1981', *Occasional Paper No. 1985/2*, ABS, Canberra.

Commonwealth Bureau of Census and Statistics 1924. *Official Year Book of the Commonwealth of Australia No. 17, 1924*, Commonwealth Bureau of Census and Statistics, Melbourne.

— 1971. *Census of Population and Housing, 30 June 1966*, Vol. 1, *Population: Single Characteristics, Part II Race*, Commonwealth Bureau of Census and Statistics, Canberra.

— 1973. 'The Aboriginal Population', *Bulletin 9, Census of Population and Housing, 30 June 1971*, Commonwealth Bureau of Census and Statistics, Canberra.

Commonwealth of Australia 1992. Tiwi Land Council, *Thirteenth Annual Report*, Tiwi Land Council, Bathurst and Melville Islands, NT.

Daly, A.E. and Smith, D.E. 1999. 'Indigenous household demography and socioeconomic status: The policy implications of 1996 Census data', *CAEPR Discussion Paper No. 181*, CAEPR, ANU, Canberra.

Daly, A.E. and Smith, D.E. 2000. 'Research methodology', in D.E Smith (ed.), *Indigenous Families and the Welfare System: Two Community Case Studies*, CAEPR Research Monograph No. 17, CAEPR, ANU, Canberra.

Ellana, L., Loveday, P., Stanley, O. and Young, E.A. 1988. *Economic Enterprises in Aboriginal Communities in the Northern Territory*, NARU, ANU, Darwin.

Finlayson, J.D. 1991. Don't Depend on Me: Autonomy and Dependence in an Aboriginal Community in North Queensland, PhD thesis, ANU, Canberra.

Gray, A. and Tesfaghiorghis, H. 1993. 'Aboriginal population prospects', *Journal of the Australian Population Association*, 10 (2): 81–101.

Henry, R. and Daly, A. 2001. 'Indigenous families and the welfare system: The Kuranda community case study, Stage Two', *CAEPR Discussion Paper No. 216*, CAEPR, ANU, Canberra.

Jonas, W. 1992. 'Aboriginal community and agency perceptions about the collection of social statistics', in J.C. Altman (ed.), *A National Survey of Indigenous Australians: Options and Implications*, CAEPR Research Monograph No. 3, CAEPR, ANU, Canberra.

King, D. 1994. *Land Use Program: Population*, Cape York Peninsula Land Use Strategy (CYPLUS), Cairns.

Loveday, P. and Wade-Marshall, D. 1985. 'Taking the 1981 Census: Aborigines in the NT', in P. Loveday and D. Wade-Marshall (eds), *Economy and People in the North*, NARU, ANU, Darwin.

McKnight, D. 1981. 'The Wik-Mungkan concept *nganwi*: A study of mystical power and sickness in an Australian tribe', *Bijdragen Tot de Taal- Land- en Volkenkunde*, 137: 90–105.

Martin, D.F. 1993. Autonomy and Relatedness: An Ethnography of Wik People of Aurukun, Western Cape York Peninsula, PhD thesis, ANU, Canberra.

— and Taylor, J. 1995. 'Enumerating the Aboriginal population of remote Australia: Methodological and conceptual issues', *CAEPR Discussion Paper No. 91*, CAEPR, ANU, Canberra.

— and — 1996. 'Ethnographic perspectives on the enumeration of Aboriginal people in remote Australia', *Journal of the Australian Population Association*, 13 (1): 17–33.

Menham, J.G. 1992. 'ATSIC's requirements for social statistics in the 1990s', in J.C. Altman (ed.), *A National Survey of Indigenous Australians: Options and Implications*, CAEPR Research Monograph No. 3, CAEPR, ANU, Canberra.

Morphy, F. and Sanders, W. (eds) 2001. *The Indigenous Welfare Economy and the CDEP Scheme*, CAEPR Research Monograph No. 20, CAEPR, ANU, Canberra.

Musharbash, Y. 2001. 'Indigenous families and the welfare system: The Yuendumu community case study, Stage Two', *CAEPR Discussion Paper No. 217*, CAEPR, ANU, Canberra.

Ross, K. 1999. 'Population issues, Indigenous Australians 1996', *ABS Occasional Paper*, Cat. No. 4708.0, ABS, Canberra.

Shergold, P. 2001. 'The Indigenous Employment Policy: A preliminary evaluation', in F. Morphy and W. Sanders (eds), *The Indigenous Welfare Economy and the CDEP Scheme*, CAEPR Research Monograph No. 20, CAEPR, ANU, Canberra.

Smith, D.E. 1991. 'Toward an Aboriginal household expenditure survey: Conceptual, methodological and cultural considerations', *CAEPR Discussion Paper No. 10*, CAEPR, ANU, Canberra.

— 1992. 'The cultural appropriateness of existing survey questions and concepts', in J.C. Altman (ed.), *A National Survey of Indigenous Australians: Options and Implications*, CAEPR Research Monograph No. 3, CAEPR, ANU, Canberra.

— (ed.) 2000a. *Indigenous Families and the Welfare System: Two Community Case Studies*, CAEPR Research Monograph No. 17, CAEPR, ANU, Canberra.

— 2000b. 'Kuranda and Yuendumu: Comparative conclusions', in D.E Smith (ed.), *Indigenous Families and the Welfare System: Two Community Case Studies*, CAEPR Research Monograph No. 17, CAEPR, ANU, Canberra.

Smith, L.R. 1980. *The Aboriginal Population of Australia*, ANU Press, Canberra.

Sutton, P.J. 1978. Wik: Aboriginal Society, Territory and Language at Cape Keerweer, Cape York Peninsula, Australia, PhD thesis, University of Queensland, Brisbane.

Taylor, J. 1993. 'Census enumeration in remote Australia: Issues for Aboriginal data analysis', *Journal of the Australian Population Association*, 10 (1): 53–69.

— 1995. Aboriginal Population Mobility in the Aurukun Region, Western Cape York Peninsula, confidential report to the Cape York Land Council, Cairns.

— 1997. 'Changing numbers, changing needs? A preliminary assessment of Indigenous population change, 1991–96', *CAEPR Discussion Paper No. 143*, CAEPR, ANU, Canberra.

— 1999. 'Aboriginal people in the Kakadu region: Social indicators for impact assessment', *CAEPR Working Paper No. 4*, CAEPR, ANU, Canberra [http//:online.anu.edu.caepr].

Young, E.A. and Doohan, K. 1989. *Mobility for Survival: A Process Analysis of Aboriginal Population Movement in Central Australia*, NARU, ANU, Darwin.

Notes on the authors

David Martin is an anthropologist and Research Fellow (part time) at the Centre for Aboriginal Economic Policy Research at the Australian National University. He has over 25 years of experience working with the Wik people of Aurukun, the location of his case study for this volume. Together with John Taylor, he has previously published an analysis of the assumptions underlying ABS census methodology, based on a comparison between the results of a census he undertook in Aurukun using ethnographic methods with those of the 1986 ABS Census conducted at the same time.

Frances Morphy has a background in anthropology and linguistics. She was a commissioning editor at Oxford University Press, Oxford before returning to Australia in 1997. She is now the academic editor and a Research Fellow (part time) in the Centre for Aboriginal Economic Policy Research at the Australian National University. She has conducted research on a variety of topics in Aboriginal communities in the Northern Territory over a period of nearly 30 years.

Will Sanders joined the North Australia Research Unit of the Australian National University in 1981. He has since held positions in the ANU's Urban Research Program, Department of Political Science and Centre for Aboriginal Economic Policy Research where he is now a Fellow. His interest in the adaptation of administrative systems to the circumstances of Indigenous people in north and central Australia also extends to the social security system and to electoral administration.

John Taylor is a Senior Fellow at Centre for Aboriginal Economic Policy Research at the Australian National University. He has been researching issues related to the enumeration of Aboriginal people in remote areas since 1986. He has a disciplinary background in geography and population studies, and is the author of numerous papers of relevance to Indigenous social and economic policy development. He is currently a member of the committee overseeing development of the ABS Indigenous Social Survey.

CAEPR Research Monograph Series

1.   *Aborigines in the Economy: A Select Annotated Bibliography of Policy-Relevant Research 1985–90*, L.M. Allen, J.C. Altman, and E. Owen (with assistance from W.S. Arthur), 1991.

2.   *Aboriginal Employment Equity by the Year 2000*, J.C. Altman (ed.), published for the Academy of Social Sciences in Australia, 1991.

3.   *A National Survey of Indigenous Australians: Options and Implications*, J.C.Altman (ed.), 1992.

4.   *Indigenous Australians in the Economy: Abstracts of Research, 1991–92*, L.M. Roach and K.A. Probst, 1993.

5.   *The Relative Economic Status of Indigenous Australians*, 1986–91, J. Taylor, 1993.

6.   *Regional Change in the Economic Status of Indigenous Australians, 1986–91*, J. Taylor, 1993.

7.   *Mabo and Native Title: Origins and Institutional Implications*, W. Sanders (ed.), 1994.

8.   *The Housing Need of Indigenous Australians, 1991*, R. Jones, 1994.

9.   *Indigenous Australians in the Economy: Abstracts of Research, 1993–94*, L.M. Roach and H.J. Bek, 1995.

10.   *The Native Title Era: Emerging Issues for Research, Policy, and Practice*, J. Finlayson and D.E. Smith (eds), 1995.

11.   *The 1994 National Aboriginal and Torres Strait Islander Survey: Findings and Future Prospects*, J.C. Altman and J. Taylor (eds), 1996.

12.   *Fighting Over Country: Anthropological Perspectives*, D.E. Smith and J. Finlayson (eds), 1997.

13.   *Connections in Native Title: Genealogies, Kinship, and Groups*, J.D. Finlayson, B. Rigsby, and H.J. Bek (eds), 1999.

14.   *Land Rights at Risk? Evaluations of the Reeves Report*, J.C. Altman, F. Morphy, and T. Rowse (eds), 1999.

15.   *Unemployment Payments, the Activity Test, and Indigenous Australians: Understanding Breach Rates*, W. Sanders, 1999.

16.   *Why Only One in Three? The Complex Reasons for Low Indigenous School Retention*, R.G. Schwab, 1999.

17.   *Indigenous Families and the Welfare System: Two Community Case Studies*, D.E. Smith (ed.), 2000.

18.   *Ngukurr at the Millennium: A Baseline Profile for Social Impact Planning in South-East Arnhem Land*, J. Taylor, J. Bern, and K.A. Senior, 2000.

19. *Aboriginal Nutrition and the Nyirranggulung Health Strategy in Jawoyn Country*, J. Taylor and N. Westbury, 2000.

20. *The Indigenous Welfare Economy and the CDEP Scheme*, F. Morphy and W. Sanders (eds), 2001.

21. *Health Expenditure, Income and Health Status among Indigenous and Other Australians*, M.C. Gray, B.H. Hunter and J. Taylor, 2002.

22. *Making Sense of the Census: Observations of the 2001 Enumeration in Remote Aboriginal Australia*. D.F. Martin, F. Morphy, W.G. Sanders and J.Taylor

For information on CAEPR Discussion Papers and Research Monographs please contact:

Publication Sales, Centre for Aboriginal Economic Policy Research, The Australian National University, Canberra, ACT, 0200

Telephone: 02–6125 8211
Facsimile: 02–6125 9730

Information on CAEPR abstracts and summaries of all CAEPR print publications and those published electronically can be found at the following WWW address:

http://online.anu.edu.au/caepr/